THE VATICAN EMPIRE

by
Nino Lo Bello

TRIDENT PRESS · NEW YORK

THE
VATICAN
EMPIRE

Contents

THE
VATICAN
EMPIRE

Some Preliminary Words

I

IN 1956, SHORTLY after moving to Rome with my wife and children to take up my duties as a business news correspondent, I was faced with a household crisis—we were without water in our apartment for twenty-eight days. Calls to Acqua Marcia, the company that supplied the water in our Piazza Bologna neighborhood, were all but futile. A few times a weary technician from Acqua Marcia came around to putter with the water governor on our balcony just off the kitchen. Each time, he left us with a tiny trickle, which stopped within hours after his departure.

As with many houses in Rome served by the Acqua Marcia water works (or to give it its full name, La Società dell'Acqua Pia Antica Marcia), the problem was in the main trunk ducts below the ground. They were too narrow. Installed nearly two thousand years earlier, the pipes once formed part of ancient Rome's aqueduct system, and were still being used to provide much of modern Rome with its water. Like other apartment buildings, ours had a series of covered receptacles on the roof, each of which corresponded to one of the apartments on the floors below. The tank for our apartment held sixty gallons of water, and it filled during the night at a speed that was determined by the water governor, which was kept under lock by Acqua Marcia. By dawn, with no one having used the faucets, the tank would usually be replenished, and for that day we would have water—provided we didn't use all sixty gallons too soon. This meant not flushing the toilet after every visit. It also meant not taking a bath in more than two inches of water.

I didn't know during those first arduous weeks that the Acqua Marcia company belonged to the Vatican.

Compounding our woes during this period was the fact that my wife's cooking activities were severely restricted. The flow of gas in our stove was so limited that only two burners functioned at the same time, and for a reasonably steady flame she had to resort to one burner. Grumbles to the gas company were of little use. We had a poor flow of gas because the pressure was low.

I didn't know then that our gas company also belonged to the Vatican.

In lodging my various complaints and pleas for help, I had to use the phone a great deal. Unhappily, my telephone suffered from a variety of speech defects. More often than not, it was impossible to understand the crackly sounds that came out of the faulty earpiece. And frequently the undulating voice at the other end of the line simply disappeared in the middle of a sentence. Nor does this take into account the many times I would suddenly be cut off by a mechanical click or an electronic tic.

I didn't know then that our telephone company was also largely controlled by the Vatican.

Later I was to discover that the building in which I

lived belonged to a front company operating for the Vatican and that the same company owned the entire block of houses on both sides of the street.

Like millions of other Roman Catholics, I had never given any thought to the Vatican and its commercial affairs. But perhaps I should have realized earlier that the Church was indeed a financial institution. I can remember now, quite vividly, the eighteen months my Uncle Angelo, an ordained priest, spent as a special visitor to the United States, serving as an adjunct assistant pastor with a church in Brooklyn. After officiating at masses on Sundays he would return to our house, where he was staying, and place his week's pay—a sackful of coins—under his bed for safekeeping. By the time he was ready to return to Italy, the floor under the bed was completely covered with bulging sacks. What he did with the money I don't know, but I do recall that my brother and I used to play with the coins, making believe the dimes, nickels, and pennies were pieces of gold. I should have realized then the importance of money to the clergy, but at that time I was too young—and by the time I was old enough, I had forgotten about *Zio Padre's* money bags.

So, until the aforementioned incidents in Rome, I had never given thought to the Vatican as a landlord, to the Vatican as a moneyed institution, to the Vatican as a nerve center for finance, to the Vatican as an organization concerned with profits and losses, assets and liabilities, receipts and expenses. The idea that the Vatican was the headquarters for big business just never occurred to me. Nor had I ever entertained the notion that the Pope might be wealthy or the notion that his church, my church, was not only a religious, charitable, and educational institution but also a tremendous financial empire.

11

The Vatican is not only in the business of selling God. Its total enterprise goes beyond God.

Secrecy surrounds the financial phases of the Vatican's operation. The only sovereign state that never publishes a budget, the Vatican is the one organized church that keeps its money affairs strictly to itself. And so ramified and complicated are those affairs that it is doubtful whether any single person, including the Pope, has a complete picture of them.

Although I had never previously questioned the Church's finances, I began, soon after the Piazza Bologna ordeals, to wonder, How rich is the Pope? Or, put another way, How much money does the Roman Catholic Church, the oldest and largest corporation in the world, possess? To be frank, I do not have an answer to this question. Nor can I state with precision how much the Vatican earns each year. Neither will I make a calculated guess as to how wealthy the pontifical empire is. On the question, How rich is the Pope?, suffice it to say that it has become increasingly clear he doesn't even know himself.

At best, this report on Vatican finances, which I have arduously pieced together during the past ten years, will reveal this venerable organization as one of the greatest fiscal powers in the world.

On the face of it, the Vatican today is vastly different from what it was a century ago. Yet it still keeps its financial operations carefully hidden behind a veil of obscurity. The fact that the Vatican has been able to maintain this secrecy in an age when business and economics are of prime interest is indeed remarkable. But at last, tiny tears in the veil are beginning to appear, and the two-thousand-year-old structure, hitherto known solely for its sacerdotal functions, is being exposed as a locus of financial power.

As employed here, the term "Vatican wealth" should not be confused with the so-called Church patrimony, which consists of churches, ancient buildings, and art treasures. The Church's art treasures, many of which are in the Vatican Museum, include literally thousands of masterpieces—paintings, sculpture, tapestries, and maps —to which no dollar amount can be assigned. Priceless indeed are such works of art as Michelangelo's *Pietà* in St. Peter's, the frescoes in the Sistine Chapel, and the paintings by Raphael in the Apostolic Palace. One could also mention the Church's invaluable collections of antiquities —gold and silver crosses, Byzantine jewelry, altar pieces, furniture, chalices and other vessels. The five hundred thousand aged volumes and sixty thousand old manuscripts in the Vatican Library are also part of the Church patrimony. Because none of the treasures will ever be put on the market, it is folly even to hazard a guess as to the cumulative worth of these items. But, conceivably, they could bring a billion dollars under an auctioneer's gavel.

In terms of the frame of reference used here, "Vatican wealth" is the money that the world headquarters of the Catholic Church is in business to make—the profits that the Vatican has assembled all its heavy artillery to pursue and protect. It is not the task of this book to expose the Church as an economic dinosaur or a hand-rubbing collection of moneylenders. Still less is the book intended to be an attack on either the papacy or the Church itself in the traditional and predictable manner of the anticlericalists. Rather, my purpose here is to explore the Vatican's relationship with the sign of the dollar, a symbol as powerful in today's world as that of the Cross. Mind you, this is not intended as criticism of the Vatican,

13

for the Vatican has every right to engage in activities from which revenue can accrue.

I shall never forget the first time I stood in a Vatican City bank and watched the tellers at work, dealing with nuns, Jesuits, missionaries, and bishops. During a quiet moment I said to one of the tellers, "I guess some of your clients, being of the religious calling, don't know very much about money."

The young man had the correct answer for this display of naïveté. "Sir," he said with adding-machine accuracy, "it is my experience that everybody knows a lot about money."

Laymen like myself have a tendency not to equate their religion, or the dedicated people who administer it, with practical, down-to-earth matters like money or economics. Yet the popes of the last hundred years have never been able to divorce themselves from these matters. Perhaps the most prophetic words ever written by a pope, as far as the Vatican's present-day position of economic strength is concerned, are those of Pius XI in a now-famous encyclical, *Non Abbiamo Bisogno* (*We Don't Have Need*). Published in France, the encyclical had to be smuggled out of the Vatican because it denounced the Fascist regime. It reads:

Immense power and despotic economic domination are concentrated in the hands of a few, who for the most part are not the owners, but only the trustees and directors of invested funds, which they administer at their own good pleasure. This domination is most powerfully exercised by those who, because they hold and control money, also govern credit and determine its allotment, for that reason supplying, so to speak, the life blood to the entire economic body and grasping in their hands, as it were, the very soul of production, so that no

14

one dare breathe against their will. This accumulation of power is the characteristic note of the modern economic order.

Pius XI was speaking of another world, in another period, yet his words have meaning when applied to the Vatican empire as it exists today. Thanks to his successors (Pius XII, John XXIII, and Paul VI) and their financial guardians, who subscribe to the theory that what's good for General Motors is also good for the Vatican, the Church is now big business.

In writing this book, I have left the well-trodden paths of theology and entered the hallways of modern economics, Vatican style. To the Vatican men who normally walk these halls, a story on the price of tin in Malaya has as much significance as the story of the moneychangers being chased out of the Temple. In gathering material for the book, it was necessary to infiltrate, like a spy, into the Vatican's deepest recesses. Contacting people within the Vatican is an experience like no other, and I can only hope that some of the excitement will rub off on the reader.

When it comes to acknowledgments for help received, I am a hopeless bankrupt, for I cannot enumerate the names of the Vatican citizens who helped me. The seal of silence will keep their identities *sine nomine perpetuus.* I feel, however, I must mention my debt to Bela von Block, Paul Gitlin, Gene Winick, Cynthia White, Joseph Wechsberg, Walter Lucas, Barrett McGurn, Bob Neville, Irving R. Levine, Bill Pepper, Corrado Pallenberg, Walter Matthew Schmidt, Ernesto Rossi, Stellina Orssola, Lidia Bianchi, Milo Farneti, William McIlroy, Avro Manhattan, and Father John Smith (not his real name), who read portions or all of the manuscript or who other-

15

wise provided assistance. I must also express my deep gratitude to my wife, Lefty. With her able and conscientious examination of the manuscripts, she has added much to improve the book and has provided more specific services than can be enumerated here. The shortcomings of the following attempt and the judgments as to matters of fact set forth remain, of course, the responsibility of the writer.

The
Pope's
Shop
II

"Offer me no money, I pray you; that kills my heart."
(Shakespeare, THE WINTER'S TALE)

"THE POPE'S SHOP"—perhaps one of the most un-complimentary expressions heard in Rome—is used by Catholics and non-Catholics alike. But unlike some other derogatory terminology employed to describe the Roman Catholic Church, the phrase *la Bottega del Papa* or *la Santa Bottega* (the Pope's Shop) was originated by the Catholics themselves. It seems to have been in use for at least five centuries.

The long-standing idea that the Vatican is in one aspect of its total personality a business concern could not exist unless it had some foundation in fact. When anticlerical Italians discuss the Vatican they are likely to shrug their shoulders and remind you that *l'oro non fa odore* (gold has no smell). The "gold" alludes not only to the gilded interiors of Italy's churches and shrines but also to the riches of the Vatican.

Devoted as most Italians are to the papacy, they have no illusions about the Vatican, its position of power in the corporation family of Italy, its affluence, or its influence. However rich the Vatican may be, and indeed there is a

17

tendency among some Italians to lose all reason on this subject, the fact stands that Italy's citizenry regard the Pope as one of the richest men in the world—not personally, but by virtue of his office, his position, his status, his power.

Devout Italians are probably the world's biggest backbiters when it comes to the Vatican's concern with fiscal matters, with cash receipts, and with dollar-sign riches. Hence they, like anticlerical Italians, speak cynically of the Pope's Shop.

The ostensible wealth of the 108.7-acre enclave inside the sturdy Leonine Walls—the magnificent church buildings, the land, the many thousands of art treasures and precious manuscripts—serves only as the visible tip of the financial iceberg. The largest chunk of the Vatican's empire lies below the surface. There it continues to grow, in spite of changing currents. Once, after World War I, the Vatican nearly went bankrupt. At every other time in its history, the Church has had a golden touch and has protected its investments wisely in almost every field of economic endeavor—not only in Italy but also in several other countries, including the United States and Canada.

One cardinal's aide quipped to me not long ago, "The Vatican should truly be judged by the companies it keeps."

In a weak moment, another elderly churchman, himself a millionaire, sighed and admitted, "Ours is a dilemma indeed: if we give the image of being too rich, people won't lend us their support; if we appear too poor, we lose their respect."

This is the same individual who related an anecdote that made the rounds behind the Vatican walls several years ago. The joke concerned the late Francis Cardinal Spellman and his business know-how. According to the story, St. Peter was giving a stately dinner. Though all of the distinguished guests had been assigned to tables, Cardinal Spellman could not locate his place. So he asked St. Peter. But St. Peter couldn't find it either. He looked among the seats reserved for cardinals. Then he remembered.

"Oh, excuse me, Your Eminence!" he apologized. "In the seating plan I had you placed with the businessmen."

It is said in Vatican circles that when Cardinal Spellman first heard the story he was greatly amused because he took the joke as a tribute to his financial acumen. Respected by Holy See officials for his business and Wall Street contacts, Cardinal Spellman did remarkably well as the official U.S. representative for an offshoot of the Vatican's financial operation which, up till the end of 1967, dealt with pontifical funds abroad. This was the office known as the Special Administration, one of four concerned with Vatican finances. Its headquarters were in a tiny room on the same floor as the Pope's private apartment. Thirteen persons, four of whom were accountants, were on its staff.

During the summer of 1967, Pope Paul began clearing away some of the centuries-old cobwebs surrounding the Curia, the central government of the Roman Catholic Church, and created, among other things, a new "ministry of finance." Designed to streamline the Church's bureaucracy, the sweeping Curia reforms gave rise, effective January 1, 1968, to the new finance office called the Prefecture of Economic Affairs of the Holy See. Combining functions previously undertaken independently by other bodies, the Prefecture now draws up an annual

19

budget for the Pope's approval, provides balance sheets for all Curia departments, and supervises all of the Vatican's economic operations. In essence, the Prefecture serves as the Vatican equivalent of a finance ministry by overseeing and coordinating activities of the various offices which handle Vatican funds.

Functioning under the Prefecture is a new office that the Pope created in the spring of 1968—called the Administration for the Patrimony of the Holy See, which combines two older financial offices, the Administration for the Goods of the Holy See (which administered the normal revenues coming into the Vatican) and the Special Administration of the Holy See (which Pope Pius XI established in 1929 to oversee the investment and use of indemnities paid to the Holy See by Italy for lands and properties seized by Italy with the fall of the Papal States in 1870).

The creation of the Prefecture eliminated, in name if not in fact, two other departments concerned with Vatican finances—the Institute for Religious Works and the Administration of the Vatican City State. But it did not abolish the so-called Administration of the Holy See Property. This organization, established in August 1878, is responsible not only for property on Vatican grounds but also for extraterritorial palaces spread all over Rome and landholdings in other parts of the world. Most of this property was left to the Holy See after the Papal States were annexed to the Kingdom of Italy during the nineteenth century.

The Administration of the Vatican City State, now defunct, handled the payroll of Holy See employees, including the Vatican's police and armed forces, and dealt with Vatican City's sanitation, medical care, public utilities, and newspaper; it also supervised the Vatican's radio station and the Vatican's astronomical observatory, the Vatican Museum, and the Vatican Library.

The Institute for Religious Works, the other Vatican fiscal appendage that was eliminated, in name if not in fact, was set up in 1942 by Pope Pius XII. It is nothing more than a bank—for taking "into custody and administering capital destined to religious work." It is situated in the Holy Office courtyard, has windows worked by tellers in priestly garb, accepts deposits, opens current accounts, cashes checks, transfers money, and carries out all other bank operations. It differs from other banks in that its depositors belong to a select group. They are the residents of the ecclesiastical state, members of the clergy who run schools and hospitals, diplomats accredited to the Holy See, and some Italian citizens who have given notable service to the Church.

The organization that through 1967 was the backbone of papal business interests and served as a kind of finance ministry was the one known as the Special Administration (now absorbed under the new setup). Established in 1929, after Fascist Italy and the Holy See had signed the Lateran Treaty [see Chapter V for a discussion of this treaty], the Special Administration took the sum of nearly $90 million granted to the Holy See by dictator Benito Mussolini as an indemnity for the loss of the Papal States and, by careful investing, increased it to about $550 million. This unconfirmed figure, at best a conservative calculation, is the one usually offered by Rome's banking fraternity and represents what is believed to have been the value of the liquid assets of the Special Administration during the closing months of 1967.

Unique because of its freedom of action, which must

have been the envy of every businessman and finance minister in the world, the Special Administration answered to no one. No elected congress or government cabinet kept tabs on it. It was not required to present reports to stockholders' meetings. Because it operated in secrecy (as does the new "ministry of finance"), no newspapers could play watchdog. In Italy and most other countries it paid no taxes. Since it worried very little about the availability of capital, it could undertake long-term programs and risks. With diplomatic privileges, its operations were often made easier, and with diplomatic contacts, which kept the "home office" regularly informed on all matters likely to have a bearing on economic trends, it had a certain edge over competitors.

The man who ran the Special Administration from the end of 1958 until its dissolution was Alberto Cardinal di Jorio, who was appointed in 1939 as an assistant in the office. In 1942, he was assigned to the Institute for Religious Works (the Vatican's bank), and, in 1944, he became its president—while he still served in the office of the Special Administration. Later, he became the secretary of the commission of three cardinals administrating this latter body. Di Jorio, who was appointed a cardinal in 1958, conducted the organization's operations with masterly prudence and surrounded himself with a brain trust of competent financiers, among whom were Luigi Mennini, an Italian layman, and the Marquis Henri de Maillardoz, a former director of the Crédit Suisse of Geneva, where the Vatican maintains at least two numbered bank accounts.

Although some funds are kept in the Crédit Suisse of Geneva, the Vatican maintains deposits in numerous public banks as well.

The late Domenico Cardinal Tardini, the Pope's Secretary of State, once maintained in a press interview that whispers about the Vatican's great wealth were exaggerated, that the image had been distorted. Yet a serious reporter who puts two and two together does not get four, or even twenty-two—but a sum that adds up to hundreds of millions of dollars.

As far as its public image is concerned, the Vatican prefers to encourage the impression that it is an organization with a modest income and huge expenditures. Vatican City does, for example, issue new stamps and special series of stamps several times a year. In this way, it is not unlike other small countries that produce and sell stamps in order to add foreign exchange to their bank accounts. Vatican stamps, however, are very much sought after, and the sales bring in close to $400,000 each year. The Vatican Museum, which charges admission, also brings in some income—but most of this is used to pay the many guards and for the maintenance of the museum itself.

Perhaps the most lucrative of the Vatican's direct sources of income is "Peter's Pence," which provides roughly $1.5 million each year, derived from contributions made in all parts of the world, wherever there are Roman Catholic churches or dioceses. A custom that developed in Britain over a thousand years ago, when a yearly tax was imposed on householders in favor of the Pope, Peter's Pence is now strictly voluntary. The English tax fell into disuse after the Reformation, but the voluntary donation was revived in the middle of the nineteenth century, when a committee formed in Paris to honor St. Peter with an annual gift. The idea was picked up in Turin, Italy, and, before long, in the United States.

Eventually it spread through Europe, then to South America, and finally all over the globe. June 29 is usually the day on which the money—donated in the name of St. Peter and St. Paul—is collected in Catholic churches everywhere. The accumulated money, Peter's Pence, then accompanies the bishops on their personal visit to the Pope. The bishops' payments are made by check, usually for U.S. dollars.

Another form of direct revenue for the Vatican comes from private contributions and legacies left by devout Catholics. This is considered by some insiders to be among the Vatican's largest sources of direct income. The amount runs into millions of dollars each year, but precise figures are impossible to obtain. More often than not, some of the money willed within a given parish or diocese remains there, and never filters through to the Vatican itself.

When money is left to a Roman Catholic parish, it becomes a matter for the Congregation for the Clergy, a Vatican-based organization that concerns itself with the day-by-day affairs of each diocese. Although it is not a part of the central financial organization of the Vatican, the Congregation is charged with numerous financial responsibilities. Primarily, it proffers advice to laymen on the adjustment of wills in favor of religious works, the acquisition of legacies and trusts, and the mortgaging of private estates, and it gives help and instruction to priests and pastors on the use and administration of Church-owned properties. In addition, the Congregation establishes the fees that are to be collected for various Church functions, like baptismal ceremonies and weddings.

When the present Pope was a young cleric known as Monsignor Montini, he served as private secretary to

Pope Pius XII and also as extraordinary secretary in charge of internal Vatican affairs. One of his jobs involved dealing with, among other financial matters, bequests. As a result of this assignment, Pope Paul knows more about the fiscal machinery of the Vatican than did any pope before him.

On the delicate subject of Vatican finances, there is a decided information gap, for persons on the inside as well as for those on the outside. The Vatican has wanted it that way. It has not wanted to organize its affairs so that any single individual could, during the course of his workday, piece together the total picture of its infinitely ramified financial operations. Apparently, only one person has been privileged to see this picture. His name was Bernardino Nogara.

Much of the credit for the Vatican's success in business after 1929 belongs to this one-time student of architecture. Bernardino Nogara demonstrated his financial genius after being entrusted by Pope Pius XI with the responsibility of administering the $90-million indemnification granted to the Holy See by Mussolini. Nogara, former vice president of the Banca Commerciale Italiana, had come to the attention of Vatican officialdom through Pope Benedict XV, who had made personal investments in Turkish Empire securities with the help and advice of Nogara, who then headed the Istanbul branch of the Banca Commerciale. Placed in charge of the newly created Special Administration, the devout Nogara had a free hand, and although he ran much of the Vatican's business out of his fedora, revealed himself as a remarkable manager of money. By undertaking a world-wide investment policy, he increased the initial capital many times over.

In pursuit of profit, Nogara abided by a self-imposed rule that the Vatican's investment program should not be hampered by religious considerations. During the early fifties, therefore, he used papal funds to speculate in government bonds of Protestant Britain, which he viewed as a better risk than the stocks of Catholic Spain, then in an economic slump. When he died late in 1958, at the age of eighty-eight, he left a "methodology" that was followed religiously by his successors, who continued to realize fantastic gains.

The mysterious Bernardino Nogara was born in Bellano, near Lake Como, in 1870—the same year that the Kingdom of Italy confiscated the last of the Papal States, the $90-million indemnification for which Nogara was later to administer. As a young man, Nogara laid aside his architectural training and worked in England, Bulgaria, Greece, and Turkey directing mine operations. During the peace negotiations with Austria, Hungary, Bulgaria, and Turkey at the end of World War I, he served as an Italian delegate on the economic and finance committee. From 1924 to 1929, he was in Berlin as an administrator on the Inter-Allied Reparations Commission, which had been entrusted with finding a solution for the problem of collecting German reparations.

A taciturn, elusive figure, Nogara was given his Vatican assignment by a pope who had little training in finance. Nogara had no obligations to show any immediate profits from his investments and was free to invest the funds anywhere in the world (with little worry about taxes). He made full use of these privileges.

He guided his actions by the reliable reports of the Vatican's world-wide network of ambassadorial representatives. Bishops and informed Catholic laymen provided intelligence—often via the Vatican's own "hot line" —that an ordinary banker could not hope to acquire at any price.

In the course of his career, Nogara had become a specialist in gold. Thus for a considerable period after he took over the Special Administration, he engaged in the trading of gold bullion for gold coins and gold coins for gold bullion in deals that, without precise details, defy understanding of anything but the fact that most of them were profitable. His confidence in the precious metal virtually unshakable, the canny Nogara spent $26.8 million to buy gold from the United States at the official rate of $35 per fine troy ounce, plus 0.25 percent for handling charges. In later years, rumors cropped up that the Vatican had obtained this gold at a special price of $34 an ounce, but when the rumors were printed in—and given some credence by—a United Nations publication, the U.S. Treasury Department dismissed the matter once and for all in April 1953, by stating that the Vatican had made the purchase at the same price as anybody else. In fact, $5 million of the Vatican-acquired gold was sold back to the United States, leaving a net sale of $21.8 million. The Vatican gold, which is in the shape of ingots, is on deposit with the U.S. Federal Reserve Bank.

A favorite Nogara ploy involved a most intricate financial maneuver, by which he manipulated the flexibility of the Vatican's Swiss bank accounts. The explanation is a bit complicated and may necessitate a second reading. Nevertheless, here it is:

Nogara would ask his Swiss bank to deposit Vatican money in New York under the Swiss bank's name. He then got the Swiss bank to order the American bank to lend dollars to an Italian firm that was owned by the

Vatican. The Italian firm, to which the money belonged in the first place, charged the interest it was paying in America to itself in the Swiss account. In this way Nogara could safely (and secretly) invest the Pope's money without any interference from the Italian authorities during those periods when currency restrictions were being imposed by the state.

Without exaggeration, it can be said that Nogara, apparently driven by deep religious motivations, used his financial wizardry to become the Vatican's "secret weapon." As a dictator of the Vatican's funds, he answered to no one—not even to the committee of three cardinals which, theoretically, supervised the functions of the Special Administration. Nor did Pius XI have any clear idea of what Nogara was doing. But the Pope had faith in Nogara, and the evidence is there that that faith was rewarded.

When Eugenio Cardinal Pacelli mounted the pontifical throne in 1939 as Pius XII, it was known that he entertained certain suspicions about Nogara—and this led to a number of rumors about the Special Administration. For one thing, it was whispered that there was virtually nothing left of the large sum of Lateran money. In one of his initial administrative acts, the new pope established a private investigating committee of cardinals who were knowledgeable in the complexities of banking and international finance. A thorough check was made.

Contrary to what many had preferred to suspect, Nogara had invested the Vatican funds wisely and shrewdly. In fact, the initial capital had increased so many times over that the Vatican was richer before the opening days of World War II than it had ever been before. After the report was in, Nogara was completely untouchable.

Few anecdotes can be told about this financial fox, for Nogara successfully managed to keep almost everything he did a secret—even from his superiors, who trusted him implicitly. A ranking Vatican official once said, "Nogara is a man who never speaks to anybody; nor does he tell the Pope much, and I would guess, even very little to God—yet he is a man worth listening to."

One Nogara incident can be reported, however. It involved a run-in with the British government. In 1948, the Catholic Relief Organization in Germany had been presented with several shiploads of wheat, purchased by the Vatican from Argentina. Nogara, attempting to pay for the wheat with British pounds he had deposited in England, ran afoul of Whitehall, for at that time England was undergoing an austerity period, with the usual currency restrictions. Annoyed, London negotiated with the Holy See, and Nogara, bending, agreed instead to invest the money he had in England in government bonds. But for the man with the golden touch, the defeat, such as it was, ended in victory. Over the long run the investment in British bonds turned out very favorably. Still, the transaction goes down on the books as one of the few in which Nogara's hand was ever forced.

After retiring in 1956 for reasons of health, Nogara continued to serve the Vatican by advising his successors in a private capacity. That he had proved himself scrupulous in the execution of his assignment, there is not the slightest doubt. That he bequeathed not only his know-how but a well-oiled, smoothly functioning piece of financial machinery, there is also not the slightest doubt. Because of the secret nature of his operations, he was given very little space in the public prints when he died in November of 1958. Yet no other single individual, pope or cardinal, ever gave as much impetus and muscle to Vatican finances as did Bernardino Nogara, the invisible man who started out to be an architect and succeeded in building a financial empire.

Perhaps the man is best summed up in a document he left for his successors. In it he enumerated his strategies. A copy of this eight-part "Nogara Credo" came into my hands and is offered herewith in translation:

1. Increase the size of your company because it will be easier to obtain funds from the capital markets.

2. Increase the size of your company because high-capacity installations allow the reduction of industrial costs and the subdivision of overall expenses.

3. Increase the size of your company because it is possible to economize on transportation.

4. Increase the size of your company because it will allow capital to be invested in scientific research that can bring tangible money results.

5. Increase the size of your company because the personnel can be organized and used in a more rational manner.

6. Increase the size of your company because fiscal controls on the part of government become advantageously difficult.

7. Increase the size of your company because it is necessary to offer the customers the best technical product.

8. Increase the size of your company because this will engender more increases.

However sanctified the name of Bernardino Nogara, not all of the Vatican's trusted employees avoided besmirching themselves. At about the time Nogara was involved with the Argentine wheat difficulty, another Vatican figure became the center of a scandal that brought severe repercussions. The financial body involved was the Administration of the Holy See Property, which had been founded in 1878 to supervise the management of Vatican-owned property.

Monsignor E. P. Cippico, a youthful prelate employed

by the Vatican Archives, got entangled in a series of financial deals that eventually brought him to ruin. The war over, many countries, including Italy, were suffering under currency restrictions. Eager to shift money to Switzerland and other countries, either for investment or for the purchase of goods for import, some Italian businessmen discovered that they could transfer funds through the Administration of the Holy See Property, for the Vatican was exempt from Italy's currency regulations. Monsignor Cippico, an extrovert who enjoyed moving in high-society circles, and who had some personal contacts in the Administration, served as a go-between for those persons who wanted to get their money out of the country. Needless to say, he was a very popular man.

All went well until Cippico ventured out on his own and agreed to underwrite the production costs of a movie on the life of St. Francis of Assisi. To cover up the outflow of money, a lot of money, Cippico enlarged his questionable operations. But the film never got past the first reel. Meanwhile, as more and more people who had entrusted him with large sums to transfer out of Italy saw nothing come of their money, the roof started to cave in on Cippico. He was arrested by the Pope's Gendarmery, made to stand a Vatican inquiry, found guilty, defrocked, and put into detention. Later he stood trial in an Italian court and was convicted of swindling; still later he was set free by a court of appeals. The persons who had entrusted money to him placed legal claims against the Vatican, and in time everyone was reimbursed.

Having learned some hard lessons in the world of business, the Vatican is now exceedingly prudent about whom it will entrust with either money or responsibility. The man appointed by Pope Paul (in January 1968) to handle the newly created Prefecture of Economic Affairs is Egidio Cardinal Vagnozzi, who had served as the Pope's top diplomat in Washington. Formerly the Apostolic Delegate to the United States for nine years, Cardinal Vagnozzi (now in his early sixties) replaced Angelo Cardinal dell'Acqua, who had been named four months earlier to the job of "finance minister."

Cardinal Vagnozzi's two septuagenarian associates in the new "ministry of finance," which will prepare the Vatican's annual budget, its first, are Joseph Cardinal Beran, Archbishop of Prague, who served sixteen years of Communist detention, and Cesare Cardinal Zerba of Italy, a theologian who served for twenty-six years as Under-Secretary and then Secretary of the Congregation of Sacraments.

Already ordained a priest at age twenty-three—thanks to a special dispensation in 1928 from the pope—Vagnozzi has spent most of his career in service abroad. Four years after his ordination, he was sent to the United States to work in the Washington office of the Apostolic Delegate. It is said that his boat trip from Italy to America may have had a significant meaning in his career, for he was accompanied across the Atlantic Ocean by the then–Monsignor Francis Spellman who had been assigned to duty in Boston. The bond of friendship and respect between the two men was to remain firm until Spellman's death recently.

Vagnozzi stayed in the United States for ten years before a transferral to Portugal, once again in the capacity as a junior counselor in the office of the Apostolic Delegate. From Lisbon he went to Paris, there to become a confidant of the then–Apostolic Delegate Angelo Roncalli (later Pope John XXIII). In 1948, Vagnozzi received an assignment to lay the groundwork in India for the exchange of ambassadors between the Delhi Government and the Holy See, and a year later he was dispatched to the Philippines as the Apostolic Delegate.

Succeeding in establishing diplomatic relations with the Republic of the Philippines in 1951, Vagnozzi became the Vatican's first ambassador (Nuncio) there and stayed in the post until 1958, at which time Pope John thought it best to send him back to the United States to fill the job of Apostolic Delegate left open by Amleto Cardinal Cicognani who had become Vatican Secretary of State. Unlike most of the previous Roman Catholic representatives in Washington, Vagnozzi—by now an avid student of Yankee culture and an admirer of the "American way of doing things"—did considerable traveling all over the fifty states, climaxing his nine-year tour of duty with a visit to Alaska to bring blessings, money and material help from Pope Paul to flood victims in Anchorage, Kodiak, and Seward in 1964.

Although he took his formal training in philosophy and theology, Cardinal Vagnozzi is a keen student of the American economy. With the help of Cardinal Spellman, Vagnozzi kept abreast of events in the business and financial world of the United States. Not without reason, therefore, is it believed that no single person inside the Vatican has the solid background and incisive knowledge of American business practice as has the Pope's new "finance minister."

Apart from the three cardinals who supervise the Vatican's wealth, the Church must also depend on its *uomini di fiducia* (men of trust), who handle the Vatican's financial interests as nonclerics. The circle of laymen who enjoy the proxy of the pope is necessarily tight because it is these few chosen trustees who most often represent the Vatican in the outside business world.

Who are some of these men, and where do they fit in the scheme of things?

A clue as to whether Vatican penetration has taken place within a given company is usually provided by the names of the members of the board of directors. Industrial corporations and holding companies often expose Church interest by listing, in one capacity or another, the names of known Vatican agents. "Agents" is perhaps not the happiest word to describe the members of the Vatican's inner lay circle, but it best indicates the purpose they serve. Whenever a "Vatican name" appears on the board of directors of a utility, for example, investigation will almost invariably bring out the fact that the Vatican holds a minor, or even a major, interest in that organization. Often the prestige of the "agent's" name gives a reporter his first indication of the extent of the Vatican's interest.

For instance, up until his resignation in the spring of 1968 from his post as special delegate of the Pontifical Commission for the State of Vatican City, the name of Count Enrico Galeazzi (who also resigned his offices as Director General of Technical Services and Director General of the Economic Services of Vatican City) appeared on many lists of directors. Wherever it did, it indicated to observers that he was serving within that company as a watchdog of Vatican interests. Count Galeazzi, however, continues his service within Vatican City by holding the office of architect of the Sacred Apostolic Palaces and regular architect of St. Peter's and as a member of the Commission for the Preservation of Historical and Artistic Monuments of the Holy See. In March 1968, Galeazzi became Director General of the Società Generale Immobiliare, the Vatican-owned construction company [which is discussed at length in Chapter VII], after having been its vice president since 1952. At this writing Count Galeazzi's name still appears on the boards of a few other companies in Italy.

Galeazzi, who was a close friend of Cardinal Spellman, owes most of his enviable Vatican career to the late New York Archbishop whom he met while the latter was stationed in Rome. It was through Cardinal Spellman, who selected him as the representative of the Knights of Columbus in Rome, that Galeazzi met Pope Pius when he was still Cardinal Pacelli and Secretary of State. By profession an engineer, Galeazzi became a trusted friend of Cardinal Pacelli, and the two went on various Vatican missions together—Buenos Aires in 1934, Lourdes in 1935, Paris and Budapest several years later, and New York and Washington shortly before Pacelli assumed the papal chair.

Under Pope Pius, Galeazzi became the acting governor of Vatican City, an office he retained until early 1968. Pope Pius also awarded him the jobs of Director General of Economic Services and of Keeper of the Sacred Fabric of St. Peter, which office made him responsible for the maintenance of Church property. Because of his fluent English, Galeazzi was often asked by Spellman to entertain his American businessmen friends in Rome; among the men Galeazzi entertained was Joseph Kennedy of Boston, father of the late President of the United States. Since Galeazzi was very close to the Pope, he could and often did help Spellman to get papal appointments. In view of the fact that Spellman made about three trips a year to Vatican City and always had a personal audience with the Pope (several times he was invited to tea, an exceedingly rare honor), the Galeazzi–Spellman friendship had no small effect on Vatican history in the postwar period. Some Romans who admire Count Enrico Galeazzi for his thoroughly dignified manner irreverently refer to him as "the Vatican's only lay Pope in history." That his name, therefore, is linked with Vatican business interests in Italy is not surprising.

Nor is it surprising that Pacelli is another "Vatican name." Should any one of the three Pacelli princes, all related to Pope Pius XII, appear in the corporate line-up of a company, it would be safe to assume the Vatican holds more than a minimum interest. Starting with the Società Generale Immobiliare, of which Count Galeazzi is now a general director and a member of the executive committee, Prince Carlo Pacelli's name appears on almost as many corporation listings as Galeazzi's. Prince Giulio Pacelli is on the board of Italgas, a company that has the concession to supply gas for thirty-six Italian cities, while Prince Marcantonio Pacelli is not only a member of the board of the Società Generale Immobiliare but is also prominently listed with the boards of many other companies.

Other Vatican names, powers to a lesser or greater degree in papal business affairs, are those of Luigi Gedda (a former president of Catholic Action), Count Paolo Blumensthil (a Secret Chamberlain of the Sword and Cloak), Carlo Pesenti (Director General of the Italcementi cement company and head of the Vatican's newly formed bank group called the Istituto Bancario Italiano), Antonio Rinaldi (vice secretary of the Apostolic Chamber and president of a private finance company called

Istituto Centrale Finanziaro), Luigi Mennini (holder of six important Vatican posts), and Massimo Spada (a lawyer and former administrative secretary of the now abolished Institute for Religious Works).

Not long ago, a formal study of the Vatican's business efficiency was undertaken by American Management Audit, an organization that has investigated the management of many businesses throughout the world. The Vatican scored exceedingly well, receiving what amounted to "straight-A" grades: 650 points out of a maximum of 700 for operating efficiency, 2,000 out of a possible 2,100 for effectiveness of leadership, and 700 out of a possible 800 for fiscal policy. Compared with those of other businesses examined, these were impressive ratings indeed. Management Audit indicated that the Vatican could teach other businesses quite a few lessons—not the least of which was that of avoiding the error of displaying "too much obvious zeal once a position of influence has been attained."

Indeed, the Vatican's efficient way of handling its business could serve as a model. Perhaps this is because of the influence of Nogara, whose shadow, a decade after his death, still looms over the financial brain trust of the present-day successor to Peter.

In a press interview shortly before his death, Cardinal Tardini dismissed reports on the extent of the Vatican's holdings. He said (as we noted earlier in this chapter) that rumors about the Vatican's wealth were exaggerated. Cardinal Tardini, who was well known to the Roman citizenry as "the priest with no fur on his tongue," then told the assembled newspapermen that in his opinion Nogara's decision to invest most of the Vatican's indemnity

37

from the Lateran Treaty in Italy instead of in other countries was regrettable.

"We thought we were helping Italy," His Eminence declared. "But instead we have been forever accused of trying to take over the Italian business world."

Behind
the
Walls
III

THE MIGHTIEST EGYPTIAN obelisk in the world stands in St. Peter's Square. Until a few short years ago, a riddle surrounded the great needle. This riddle has now been solved by admirable scholarly deduction.

The Emperor Caligula, whose reign ended in A.D. 41, had had the obelisk placed in the center of an arena where gladiators fought and charioteers raced, and at the base of the obelisk he had had engraved in Latin a dedication to his mother, Agrippina. In the sixteenth century Pope Sixtus V had the obelisk, which weighs 320 tons, lugged from the site of the ancient arena to its present position in St. Peter's Square. But where was the obelisk before it was in the arena? Where did it originally come from?

Since the elongated monument bears no Egyptian hieroglyphics, nobody was able to figure out its early history—until Professor Filippo Magi, an archeologist, deciphered an inscription that wasn't there and unlocked a mystery which was centuries old.

One morning, while gazing at the Latin inscription,

Professor Magi began to wonder why it had been carved on an indented rectangle and not directly on the surface of the obelisk. In the slanting rays of the morning sun, he noticed that scattered among the Latin words were innumerable little holes, each about a quarter of an inch deep. Examining the tiny holes more closely, the professor had a hunch. Could these holes be really only "bottoms" of holes that were once deeper? Could they be what remained of holes originally drilled an inch into the granite—holes in which the teeth of bronze letters of a previous inscription had been imbedded and fixed with hot lead? Perhaps, Professor Magi theorized, when Caligula received the giant stone from Egypt, he had ordered the letters removed to make room for his own inscription.

The problem now facing the archeologist was whether he could reconstruct the original bronze letters by calculating from the positions of the holes. Because many of the letters seemed to have been attached by three teeth instead of two, Professor Magi felt he stood a good chance of identifying their shape. He could then, he decided, use guess work—and the principles of cryptography—to find out what the other letters were.

Professor Magi had scores of fake plastic letters made to size. He juggled them around, and around. Then, finally, they fell into order, and the obelisk's original inscription could be read. It revealed that the obelisk had been put up in Heliopolis by Caius Cornelius Gallus, a Roman prefect to Egypt who erected many such monuments to his own glory before he fell into disfavor and died by his own hand in 27 B.C.

The story of Professor Magi's archeological detective work is one incident in the history of the obelisk. Another took place in 1586, when the obelisk was being installed in St. Peter's Square. Thousands of workers and hundreds of horses were struggling with beams, ropes, and scaffolding to lift the unwieldy seventy-five-foot monument skyward. So the engineers would not be distracted, the death penalty was ordered for any spectator who even so much as uttered a word. But friction was beginning to burn the ropes, and it appeared the monolith would fall to the ground. A sailor who was watching knew what to do. Should he risk his life by disobeying the order of silence?

"Throw water on the ropes!" he yelled at last.

The suggestion was followed, and the workers completed the job without mishap. Instead of being executed, the sailor earned a papal reward, the right to supply St. Peter's Church with palms on Palm Sunday. His heirs still have the concession today.

The giant obelisk, which is one of Rome's landmarks, is not really in Rome, or in Italy. It stands just over the Italian border, about ten yards away from Rome, which entirely surrounds the State of Vatican City. Very little is known by the outside world about this tiny country, which, although it is an artificial state, is still a sovereign one.

The State of Vatican City, the most singular community in the world, doesn't even have as many citizens as the United States Congress has members. Nor is there much prospect that Vatican City will substantially increase its population, because most of its citizens (who are clergy) do not marry. This partially explains why the death rate is forty times higher than the birth rate. There are fewer than 530 citizens within Vatican City, and altogether about nine hundred people live within its diamond-shaped seventeen-square-mile confines.

41

Unlike other nations, the State of Vatican City has no significant industry, no agriculture, and no natural resources, yet it ranks among the richest countries of the world. Millions of people cross its borders every year without a visa or any red tape, but Vatican City is the best guarded and most effectively sheltered country anywhere. The tourists who visit it never find overnight lodging, for the country doesn't have a hotel. Neither does it have a single restaurant, movie house, or legitimate theater.

Getting around this minuscule territory is difficult, especially for a stranger, because all but one of the thirty streets and squares are without street signs. There are no traffic lights, but there hasn't been an auto accident in over forty-five years. Vatican City has no streetcars or buses. Not only does the country lack hotels, restaurants, theaters, street signs, traffic lights, and public transportation, it also has no barber shop, no laundry, no dry cleaner, and not a single newsstand. Nor does it have any kind of hospital, a garbage collection crew, or a school for children.

The absence of these features is amazing, but Vatican City has other unique qualities, which may seem even more amazing.

Vatican City, a country that is managed by men of Italian origin, has a national anthem that was written by a Frenchman (Charles Gounod). The country's official language is Latin, usually considered dead. The head of state is not only the country's chief executive, he is also its legislature and judiciary, all in one, but he is neither a dictator nor a despot. The Lilliputian country has its own postage stamps and issues its own coins, yet it uses Italian money as its legal tender and depends on Italy to transport its air mail. (Local mail delivery is not made easier by the absence of any street addresses in Vatican City, but this doesn't faze the postman, who knows where everybody lives.) Vatican coins, which are the same size as the equivalent Italian coins, have the Pope's head engraved on them and usually bear a motto. "This is the root of all evil" is the translation of one such motto; "It is better to give than to receive," the translation of another.

The Vatican flag, which consists of two equal vertical stripes of yellow and white with the papal tiara above two crossed keys on the white stripe, would be recognized by few people if they saw it. Vatican license plates bear the letters S.C.V. (for *Stato Città Vaticano*) in either red or black on a white background; the numbers run from 1 to 142. The Pope has ten private cars, and these are parked in the Apostolic Stable, which was once used for papal horses. All told, there are a half dozen gasoline pumps in the Vatican, all of them carrying the same brand of gas—Esso. So far as is known, the Vatican does not plan to let Madison Avenue exploit the fact that the Pope has a tiger in his tank.

Although the country has its own railroad, there is no regular train schedule. The double-track spur enters the country through a metal gate in the Vatican wall; freight trains with supplies for the country come in fairly often, but not regularly. Mussolini put up the stone terminal building as a gift, and when the railroad was inaugurated, one of the engineers in charge of the works, offering an apology to Pius XI because the tracks had not yet been properly connected with the Italian network, assured him that that would be done shortly.

"It seems," remarked the pontiff, smiling, "that you are in a hurry to get rid of me."

43

In actuality passenger trains rarely depart from the station. The last one left the Vatican in October 1962, carrying Pope John and some members of his staff to Loreto and Assisi to offer prayers for the Ecumenical Council.

Many of the citizens of Vatican City, none of whom is subject to Italian income taxes (citizens do pay the Vatican an annual tax, but it's only 300 lire—48 cents), live in Italy rather than on Vatican ground. This is their preference. Vatican gates close at 11:30 P.M. A resident who wants to go, say, to the opera, must get special permission and must then arrange to get back inside the country after the gates close. An alien who accepts a dinner invitation to a Vatican home must leave the country before the frontier shuts down.

Since there is no privately owned real estate in Vatican City, the people who live there, not all of whom are citizens, have their quarters assigned to them. Citizens are not charged for electricity or telephone service, and rents are very low, usually about 4 percent of an individual's income. Thus a monsignor with a salary of $300 a month will usually pay about $12 a month for his assigned apartment.

Economic pressures and other problems of an industrialized society do not exist in Vatican City, even though incomes are low. Some cardinals receive as much as $800 a month; the commanding officer of the Swiss Guards gets about $340; and the editor of the unofficial Vatican daily paper also gets about $340.

A visitor once asked Pope John, "Holy Father, how many people actually work in the Vatican?"

"Oh, about half of them!" the Pope jestingly replied.

That would be about fifteen hundred people, for, altogether, about three thousand have jobs inside the Vatican.

Although most prices within the Vatican walls on items of food are concomitant with those of the neighboring country, and geared to Rome's accelerated cost of living, general expenses are much lower. Vatican housekeepers, at least half of whom are males, do most of their grocery shopping on the grounds—but it's necessary to go into Rome for such things as clothing, electrical appliances, and other durable goods. Sources in Rome supply the Vatican with its water and its electric power, while the Vatican's so-called sanitation system empties into the Roman sewers. Without the help and good will of Italy, and especially of Rome, the non-self-sufficient Vatican would be unable to function efficiently.

The State of Vatican City doesn't have a residential sector, as such. The Pope and members of his official family live in the Apostolic Palace, a conglomeration of buildings built, for the most part, during the Renaissance. With some 990 flights of stairs and more than 1,400 rooms (overlooking twenty courtyards), the palace of the Vatican is perhaps the world's largest, surpassed or matched only by the palace of the Dalai Lama in Tibet.

The Pope's nineteen-room apartment on the top floor faces St. Peter's Square. His private office, with three great recessed windows overlooking the square, is commodious and impressive. Draped in gold damask, the windows are seldom covered by curtains, for, whenever the sunlight beats in, the white slats on the inside shutters are closed. The papal work chamber measures sixty by forty feet. The floor is carpeted, and the walls are panelled in blond wood. There are tables and satin-covered chairs spaced around the room, and books fill every inch of space in the two six-foot-high, glass-enclosed cabinets.

About five feet away from the door is the Pope's desk, a table with a single center drawer. On the right side of the desk, the Pope keeps an ornate desk clock, a high-necked desk lamp with carved statuettes at the base, a roll-blotter, and several reference books, among which are the current *Pontifical Annual* and an indexed Bible. Facing the papal desk are two high-backed chairs that match the chair on which the Pope sits. Pope Paul has an electric typewriter, which he uses with consummate skill. He likes to do his own typing at night, when things are quiet. When he wants to make an appearance from his office, usually on Sundays for a noonday blessing, he invariably goes to the middle window.

On the lower floors are the apartments of the Cardinal Secretary of State and the Master of Pontifical Ceremonies. The palace also houses, in one of its extensions, the Vatican Museum, which contains what many experts believe to be the world's finest collection of ancient and classical art. The museum has the most important single art spectacle anywhere—the Sistine Chapel, in which the enormous "Last Judgment" of Michelangelo covers the entire wall behind the altar and flows onto the ceilings and upper walls, done in fresco.

Alongside the Apostolic Palace, members of the Swiss Guards have their own barracks and apartments. Vatican City has three comparatively new apartment buildings, erected to partially correct a housing shortage, which still exists. There are three cemeteries in the Vatican, but these are rarely used today, for Vatican City also has a shortage of burial places (except in the vaults of St. Peter, which are now reserved for popes).

A walk through the fenced-in Vatican Gardens, which are manicured the year around by a staff of twenty, is an unforgettable experience. There are fruit trees, cauliflower patches, plants rooted in oversized ceramic jars, and fountains of all shapes. To ensure an adequate water supply, Pius XI had 9,300 irrigators installed. Fifty-five miles of pipe lines were laid, and two reservoirs built. Each reservoir holds 1.5 million gallons of water, which comes directly from Lake Bracciano, outside Rome.

At the Pope's request, the irrigation system was equipped with some rather special devices—trick devices squirted great jets of water at the unwary visitor. When in a playful mood the Pope loved to drench new cardinals whom he inveigled to walk with him through the gardens. The jets are no longer working, but they can be seen if you know where to look.

The Vatican Gardens were one of Pius' pet projects, and he frequently let the children of Vatican employees play in them. One day, noticing a school of flashy red fish swimming in one of the small ponds, he said to the youngsters who were standing nearby, "So many cardinals— and no pope!"

The next day two boys and a girl, giggling, went to the pond and emptied the contents of a small pail into it. Later, when Pius went out for his stroll in the garden, he saw one extra fish in the pond. The fish was all white, like a pope.

Not far from the gardens is the so-called business district of Vatican City. Located to the right of St. Peter's Square, it can be reached by entering through the Santa Anna Gate, which is supervised by the Swiss Guards. Each visitor to the business district must state the nature of his business to the guardsman on duty before he is allowed to proceed. The roadway from the Santa Anna Gate leads past the tiny parish church to the grocery store, the post office, the car pool and garage, the press office, and the offices of *L'Osservatore Romano,* the Vatican's daily newspaper.

As an independent state, Vatican City has certain prerogatives with respect to Italy. For instance, in time of war Vatican citizens and personnel are given access across Italian territory. The Vatican is exempt from customs regulations, a privilege that has sometimes been abused. After the end of World War II, visitors to Vatican City began picking up cartons of American cigarettes there, taking them into Italy, where American cigarettes were hard to find, and selling them for double what they paid. As much as this rankled officials of the Italian government (which has a state monopoly on the sale of tobacco), nothing could be done. Or can be done, for the practice continues even to this day—in spite of the fact that the Vatican now rations tobacco and other items, like liquor, which sell at higher prices in Rome.

Maintaining law and order is no problem for the Vatican, which has almost no crime. No instance of a holdup on Vatican ground has ever been recorded. Some years ago, however, there was one case of housebreaking. Only two murder attempts have ever been recorded. In one case a Swiss Guardsman, in a moment of temper, wounded his commanding officer, not too seriously; in the other a demented woman shot down a priest in St. Peter's.

The Vatican prison was closed not long ago because of lack of use; it stood vacant for a while; then it was converted into a warehouse. Few inmates served any time at all in the prison. One was a clergyman, Monsignor E. P. Cippico, who had been involved and convicted of the illegal money traffic described in Chapter II. Another inmate, a man caught stealing in St. Peter's (the crime occurred more than twenty years ago), was sentenced to six months, primarily to spare him what would have been a heavier sentence from the Italian courts. He served his full term and, according to Vatican sources, enjoyed it considerably because he was very well treated, and also, "because the window to his cell overlooked the beautiful scenery of the Vatican Gardens and allowed him to breathe the gardens' balmy air."

Most of the policemen who work in the Vatican are laymen, as are the firemen, lawyers, stenographers, sales personnel, carpenters, bakers, gardeners, bricklayers, painters, mechanics, and other employees who keep the Vatican machinery functioning. To supplement this lay staff, a number of small religious societies provide services of various types. For instance, the Vatican telephone system and local mail deliveries are handled by the friars of the Little Work of Divine Providence. A group of nuns, affectionately known as the Sisters of Tapestry, specializes in the mending and restoration of the thousands of precious tapestries that adorn the walls of the Apostolic Palace. The Do Good Brothers operate the Vatican pharmacy, and on a nearby island in the Tiber, administer a hospital, where during the Nazi occupation of Rome they earned a reputation for hiding American and British pilots shot down in combat, refugee Jews, and other enemies of Hitler.

Another religious group, the Sons of St. John Bosco, provides the Vatican with typesetters and linotype operators. Charged with printing secret and confidential Vatican documents, the members of this group also run the Vatican Polyglot Printing Plant, which, as its name implies, issues publications in a variety of languages. A large

49

variety, for the Polyglot Printing Plant works with 120 different alphabets and publishes documents in hieroglyphics, Chinese ideographs, Braille, Glagolitic, Hebrew, Arabic, and Coptic.

Perhaps the most unusual job in the Vatican—a job that very few people ever hear of—is performed in a high-ceilinged room in the Apostolic Palace. The room is lined with shelves and drawers containing ashes, slivers of bones, and other remains of early saints and martyrs. Under an electric lamp in one corner of this strange chamber, the world's most macabre library, sits a Vatican officer surrounded with tiny boxes and envelopes addressed to all parts of the globe. These are for the purpose of conveying saintly relics. According to canon law, a relic must be enclosed in every altar of every church. Because churches are inaugurated each week, and an authentic relic is required for each new altar, the librarian is constantly busy filling envelopes with pinches of dust. The envelopes are sent out as registered letters.

The visitor to the Vatican is not likely to see the relic mailer at work, but no matter where he goes inside the narrow plot of land, he is likely to come across someone busily doing an unexpectedly ordinary job. The Pope's shoemaker, for example. Since 1939, the task of making papal shoes has belonged to Telesforo Carboni, who habitually refers to Paul VI as "an eight and a half narrow" and the late Pope John as "a wide ten."

Like many other shoemakers, Carboni is quite a raconteur, particularly on the matter of footwear. Once Carboni said to me, "I remember the time Pope John, who had a big foot, which could take even a ten and a half, came to me and said, 'Signor Carboni, you must make me a pair of shoes that are nice and big and don't cramp my feet.'

"A man with cramped feet, you know, will usually have cramped ideas in his head, and so His Holiness wanted a pair of shoes that wouldn't cramp him in his work. Do you follow?

"The Pope didn't have corns on his feet, but he did have a high instep, and the top of a shoe, if it was a bad fit, could cut his foot when he walked. He showed me the most comfortable pair of shoes he ever had, made by his nephew, a shoemaker in Bergamo, and they were dyed purple. I was horrified at the color. Who ever heard of a pope wearing purple shoes?

" 'Holy Father,' I said, 'you can't wear purple shoes. It's not the pope's color.'

"Pope John thought for a bit, then he said, 'But, Signor Carboni, I don't want to hurt my nephew's feelings. When I write him, I must tell him I am wearing the shoes he made for me.'

" *'Ci penso io,'* I said. 'We will color the shoes red.'

" *'Benissimo!'* exclaimed His Holiness. 'You have solved my problem. You are a saint. You have made the first miracle of my reign!' "

How the Vatican
Succeeded in Business
Without Really Trying
IV

IF THERE IS one common quality of popes it is that they are, necessarily, lonely men. Several popes have commented on their loneliness. In a rare moment of candor, Pope Paul VI made this loneliness clear to some guests during a private audience. "Some people think," he said, "that a pope lives in an atmosphere of superior serenity, where everything is beautiful, everything is easy. . . . But it is also true that the pope has cares, coming from his human littleness, which he faces every moment. This sometimes conflicts with his duties, his problems, his responsibilities. This is a distress which sometimes tastes of agony."

Pope Pius IX, one of the loneliest and least fortunate popes in all Vatican history, must indeed have tasted agony when he had to face, all but alone, the loss of more than two thirds of the Vatican's landholdings and when, after Rome was taken, he went into voluntary "exile" behind the Leonine Walls. Let us trace those dusty events, for they bear heavily on the theme of this book.

After 1815, when the Congress of Vienna restored the papal lands, which for years had been part of Napoleon's empire, the Vatican found itself with a Brobdingnagian parcel of land that sheared completely through the middle of the peninsula and separated the six Italian states. These states, or duchies, were a political reality that had for centuries made Italy nothing more than a "geographical expression." The so-called Papal States, some of which came into the Vatican's possession through donation (mostly before the ninth century) and some through the sixteenth-century conquests of Cesare Borgia (son of Pope Alexander VI), and which, several times in their history, were curtailed and abolished, consisted of some 16,000 square miles that included a population of a little over three million inhabitants in the regions of Latium, Umbria, the Marches, and Emilia-Romagna—a territory sprawling across the peninsula from the Tyrrhenian Sea to the Adriatic, bounded on the northwest by the Kingdom of Lombardo-Venetia, southeast by the Kingdom of Naples, and west by the Grand Duchy of Tuscany and the Duchy of Modena.

Papal rule over this territory was inefficient. The people who lived in it were Roman Catholics, but they did not like the idea of being governed by priests. Although taxes were light, almost nonexistent, industry and commerce were entirely undeveloped; most of the people lived by begging. On more than one occasion foreign soldiers had to be called in to bring order to sectors where disturbances had broken out. When Pope Pius IX assumed office in 1846, he made a strong effort to introduce reforms—but the Pope was not a man of the world, nor did he have political gifts and economic know-how. During the first twenty-four months of his reign, Pius IX made concessions that upset many of his cardinals. Tariffs were lowered, and commercial treaties were signed with other nations; railways were constructed; the law courts were reorganized, and local councils were set up.

But the Pope was destined to fail as a temporal sovereign. With the coming of the Risorgimento (Italy's unification movement), Pope Pius could not continue to hold the Papal States, which are now comprised within the provinces of Bologna, Ferrara, Forlì, Ravenna, Pesaro and Urbino, Ancona, Macerata, Ascoli-Piceno, Perugia, Rome, and Benevento. But for the intervention of French armies, this land would have been lost much earlier. When the Kingdom of Italy was formed in 1860, the Papal States were reduced to 4,891 square miles (with a population of about 692,000) to include the Comarca of Rome, the legation of Velletri, and the three delegations of Viterbo, Civitavecchia, and Frosinone. In September 1870, however, when the Franco-Prussian War forced France to withdraw its garrisons from papal soil, Italian troops marched into Rome and terminated the temporal power of the Pope.

Refusing to recognize the *fait accompli,* Pius voluntarily made himself the "prisoner" of the Vatican. For the next fifty-nine years the popes who followed Pius IX —Leo XIII (1878–1903), Pius X (1903–1914), Benedict XV (1914–1922), and Pius XI (1922–1939)— also enclosed themselves in voluntary captivity in the Vatican. This self-imprisonment kept the so-called Roman Question alive for over half a century; not until the signing of the Lateran Treaty in 1929 did the Vatican accept compensation for its territorial loss. Only then did the long exile behind Vatican walls come to an end.

Not much can be said about the Vatican's financial

situation from 1815 to 1929, for very little is known about this era. However, it appears that in 1848 the Papal States had, by good sense and economy, brought about a balance between receipts and expenditures. But, according to an obscure statement published by a Father Chamard in the *Annales Écclésiastiques,* this equilibrium was apparently upset in 1859.

"Without doubt," wrote Father Chamard, "from a financial point of view, the intervention of France in the settlement of the pontifical debts has diminished the annual charges, but it should not be forgotten that even after the settlement, the papal treasury still has to pay out in interest $4,267,542. If to this sum is added the ensemble of expenses calculated for 1869 at $7,848,485, the total sum arrived at passes $12,000,000. But the ordinary resources of the Sovereign Pontiff cannot support more than half this sum. Therefore $6,000,000 is the amount the faithful must supply."

To help the Vatican meet its expenses, the voluntary contribution known as Peter's Pence was revived in the United States in 1868, when the second Plenary Council of Baltimore decreed that a collection be taken up for the pope once a year in all American churches. Announcing the restoration of the tax, Herbert Cardinal Vaughan made some frank disclosures about the Vatican's financial position:

The financial condition of the Holy See from the date of the return of the Pope from Gaeta to the year 1859 has become each year more satisfactory. . . . But in the month of September 1859, Pius IX was despoiled of two thirds of his states. The Romagna, or fifteen provinces, were invaded and annexed to Piedmont. By this act the revenue of the Holy See, which had been 54,000,000 francs (or £2,100,000, or $10,800,000), was reduced to 28,000,000 francs. This might

55

still have sufficed both for the administration of the five remaining provinces and for the government, but for the debt.

The debt amounted to 24,000,000 francs a year. It had been contracted on behalf of all the provinces making up the Papal States. To the fifteen provinces annexed by Piedmont belonged 18,000,000 to 19,000,000 of the interest to be paid, as their fair proportion. The robber, however, refused to take over the burdens with the stolen provinces. . . .

Within six weeks of the occupation of the Romagna by the Piedmontese a cry for Peter's Pence had arisen in England . . . exactly three centuries after it had fallen away under Elizabeth. . . .

The sum total in Peter's Pence paid into the apostolic chamber from the end of 1859 to the end of 1865 was 45,600,000 francs. Nearly the whole of this sum was, we know from the note of M. de Corcelle, the French ambassador in Rome, employed in payment of the debt and in meeting the deficit created in the papal treasury by the Piedmontese invasion. Considerable sums continued to be collected and laid at the feet of Pius IX up to the last year of his reign. . . . On the accession of our Holy Father, Pope Leo XIII, fabulous reports were circulated as to the wealth accumulated in Peter's Pence. This was done by enemies of the Church to deceive the people and dry up the stream of their loving gifts. But the fact is that the small sum which had been invested has again and again been diminished during the last two years in order to meet the absolute necessities of the Holy See.

But, you may perhaps inquire, What are the actual necessities of the Holy See?

The actual necessities of the Holy See are the actual requirements of Christendom. It is therefore for Christendom to meet them. . . . The actual income of the Holy See, derivable from permanent and settled sources, is said to have been reduced by spoliation to £60,000. . . . Finally, as to the personal expenses of the Holy Father, they form a sum so insignificant as to be absolutely inappreciable in the general expenditure. Personally sparing and truly mortified, his habits are those of a tertiary of the poor and humble St. Francis.

Coming now to the income actually required, it has been estimated that the smallest sum that will suffice for the Holy See and the central government of the Church is about £350,000. It is said that all told about five thousand persons, including old *impiegati* [employees], are dependent upon the Holy See. The sum we have mentioned, if divided equally, would not afford to each of these the wages of a common English mechanic, while leaving nothing for the Pope's privy purse, for household expenses, for diplomatic expenses, for fabrics, for libraries, for offices, for printing and stationery, and for other inevitable incidental charges.

Whether the sum finally collected from the Peter's Pence of 1868 sufficed was never made known. But in July of 1870, the Vatican floated a loan of $200,000 from the House of Rothschild. Estimates at the turn of the century indicated that the Vatican needed $4 million a year to make ends meet.

During this period, the Vatican had its then-usual sources of income. There were monies from direct taxation—that is to say, from fees attached to various functions like marriages, baptisms, and funerals. The sale of official stamped paper for documents always brought in some revenue. Also there were legacies (which in some instances reached astonishing sums). There were also gifts that came from pilgrims in Rome; some pilgrimages brought groups of a thousand or more men and women, each of whom by tradition would leave a gift of money, never less than a dollar from American visitors. These small gifts added up. Another important contribution to the Vatican treasury in those days came from the domains of Assisi, Loreto, and Padua, from which land taxes were exacted. A percentage of the offerings received at the Shrine of Lourdes also helped fill the Pope's coffers. Masses were sold (to mitigate the purgatorial sufferings of the dead), as were relics (articles of saints' clothing, eating utensils saints had used, etc.), as were images of the Madonna, as were candles and rosaries—and pieces of straw from the straw bed of the self-imprisoned Pope

Pius IX. Coupons—repayable in heaven—were sold. And last but not least, there was the sale of annulments.

But this income wasn't enough, apparently. Several times before the signing of the Lateran Treaty, the Vatican had to dispose of some of its properties in Rome in order to meet expenses and deficits. In 1880, to give Pope Leo XIII a helping hand, a group of noblemen whose families had been closely allied to the Church for centuries founded a bank, the Banco di Roma, on behalf of the Vatican. With capital supplied by the friendly aristocracy, the Banco di Roma mostly concerned itself with the acquisition of real estate. In 1882, the bank bought the controlling interest in an English company that supplied water to Rome, and the company changed its name to La Società dell'Acqua Pia Antica Marcia. The Vatican eventually took over the company, and ran it until 1962, when most of its aqueducts, mains, tubes, pipes, and equipment were sold to a private syndicate. In 1885, the Banco di Roma bought control of Rome's trolley and bus system, too. But, by 1898, the bank had twice been forced to reduce its capitalization and was close to failing. It barely managed to survive until Bernardino Nogara intervened and put it back on its feet.

The lack of business know-how exemplified in the operation of the Banco di Roma kept the Vatican just about barely even for the half century before World War I. But, despite financial slumps with which none of the popes seemed able to cope, the Vatican chose not to make public its financial position.

Somehow, the Vatican managed to keep afloat during World War I, but after the war the Vatican was still trying to learn how to swim in the swirling currents of twentieth-century economics. In 1919, the Pope sent a representative to the United States to negotiate a loan believed to be in the vicinity of $1 million. But the Vatican apparently went about it in the wrong way, and the loan never materialized. The Vatican was rescued, however—by the Knights of Columbus, which that year had planned a pilgrimage to Rome. The visiting delegates brought with them a gift to the Pope of approximately $250,000. As far as the public record is concerned, the only other time in history that the Pope engaged in money-raising negotiations was in 1928, when a Vatican loan of $1.5 million was floated through George Cardinal Mundelein; the loan was backed by Church property in Chicago worth several million dollars.

Financially, the Vatican was in trouble after World War I. But very few people knew about it. By 1922, when Pope Benedict XV died, the papacy was well-nigh bankrupt. Like all of his predecessors, Benedict had been generous. But, unlike his predecessors, Benedict had no idea how much money he was giving out to charity. When he assumed the pontifical chair in 1914, he made no attempt to find out how much was in the apostolic sugar bowl. Benedict gave out money faster than the Vatican machinery could bring it in. In his desk drawer the Pope kept huge sums, and he would hand money freely to any priest who came to him with a tale of woe. The over-generous pontiff also made personal contributions for the creation of schools, convents, missionary settlements, and the like. Never did he give a thought to where the money was coming from.

A seemingly authentic story is told about Benedict's meeting with a bishop who was then engaged in building a convent in Palestine. The bishop, visiting Benedict on other matters, had been warned by papal advisors not to mention the project to His Holiness because there was no more "loose change" in the pontifical desk drawer. Thus the bishop talked to the Pope on general subjects—the number of conversions achieved in Palestine, the position of the Catholic religion in the Middle East, and so on. When at last it came time for the bishop to leave, Benedict said to him, "And what of your convent?"

The bishop stammered and managed to say that the building was coming along slowly, but just fine.

"In that case," said Benedict, "we shall contribute." He opened up the center drawer, where he usually kept his pin money and after foraging around found nothing, smiled, pulled open a bottom drawer on the side of the desk, and dumped out the contents. "Here," he said, "take this!" and handed the bishop $6,250.

If Pope Benedict was a flop as a manager of money, his successor, Pius XI, was possibly even more of a flop. The day after Pius XI took office, he presented the sum of $26,000 to the German cardinals to help countrymen who had suffered when the value of the mark declined. A few months later, still having made no accounting of how much money was in the Vatican treasury, Pius handed out $62,500 for a sanatorium at Thorenc, France. In the same year he also contributed $156,250 to help Russia, then opened up his purse once again and presented the poor people of Rome with $9,375. He also gave $50,000 to the victims of the Smyrna fire, $12,500 to the Catholic Institute at Cologne, and $3,125 to the Perretti Institute. The next year, 1923, Pius XI contributed $81,250 for hungry Germans, $21,875 to the Viennese, and $20,000 for Japanese earthquake victims.

Such prodigality had to lead to a day of reckoning. And it came when Monsignor Dominique Mariani, a secretary of the cardinals' committee for the management of the Holy See's property, made an inventory and discovered that the Vatican was virtually broke. Given the title *Monsignor Elemosiniere Segreto,* Mariani instituted some reforms, always with the Pope's blessing, and every Thursday would sit down with His Holiness and go over the expenses of the past week, down to the tiniest detail. For the first time in Vatican history, a common-sense bookkeeping system was instituted.

Through the efforts of Mariani, the Vatican began to face the problem of its deficits. The first audit in Church history, made in 1928, showed that the Vatican's expenses in a given day often came to $5,000. Fortunately, they were covered by income. To all intents and purposes, the Vatican was down to its bottom dollar that year, but the audit did turn up a "lost" $55,000, which saved the day.

The 1928 *Pontifical Annual* made the following brief report on the new measures being taken to reorganize the Vatican's household economy:

His Holiness Pius XI . . . has reformed the administration of Vatican finances. The entire administration of the Apostolic Palace is placed under the control of a commission of cardinals. The gifts of the faithful brought to Rome by the bishops are a sum kept apart, administered by the personal control of the Pope, paid by a person of confidence who keeps a book in which are marked all receipts and expenses, and which is balanced at the end of each week. Expenses figure annually about $1,052,631. The bookkeeping is carried out according to the most modern principles and is severely controlled.

The Vatican was beginning to take control of its financial affairs, but another problem loomed during the late nineteen-twenties to cause the Pope distress. Relations between the papacy and the Mussolini regime had deteriorated to a state of reciprocal distrust and outright hostility. There were so many conflicts between the Red Velvets of Pius and the Black Shirts of Il Duce that a volume would be necessary to detail them all. In one speech Mussolini wryly reminded everyone, "It must be understood that between the Italian State and the Vatican City there is a distance which can be measured in thousands of miles, even if it requires only five minutes to go and see it and ten minutes to walk around its confines."

Yet Mussolini, who had been called a devil by the Pope, was to do more for the Vatican than any man, any cleric, any pope, in all history. Perhaps Mussolini himself wrote the best footnote on this subject. In an article written for the French newspaper *Figaro,* he stated, "The history of Western civilization from the time of the Roman Empire to our day shows that every time the state clashes with religion, it is always the state which ends defeated."

These words were written after 1929, the year in which Italy signed the Lateran Treaty, and helped create for the Vatican the best of all possible worlds.

The
Lateran
Treaty
V

"Mussolini was the man sent by Providence."

(Pope Pius XI)

AN EXTREMELY SUPERSTITIOUS man, and quite un-
ashamed of it, Benito Mussolini, who ruled Italy with
an iron hand from 1922 until 1943, often during public
appearances unabashedly put his hand into his pocket to
tap his private parts for good luck. He believed the gesture would protect him in case someone in his presence
had the "evil eye." Mussolini had some other questionable beliefs. He gave credence to the ill effects of the cold
light of the moon upon the face of a sleeping man and to
the prognostications of fortune-tellers and palm readers.
Swayed though he was by the occult sciences, Mussolini
never believed in God, nor, except for political convenience, did he ever call himself a Catholic.

Yet no man did more for the Vatican than did the
Italian dictator. When he signed the Lateran Treaty with
the Pope on February 11, 1929, he gave the Church a
"shot in the arm" that proved to be critical in its economic history. Generally speaking, many people know *of*
the Lateran Treaty, but very few know *about* it—why it
came about, what its provisions were, and how it pro-

vided the Church with the springboard it needed to jump into Italy's economy. If politics alone can be said to make strange bedfellows, then politics mixed with religion produces associations that defy characterization. Such was that of Il Duce and the Pope at the end of the nineteen-twenties.

Why did these two previously incompatible individuals, with their incompatible ideas, undergo a wedding of sorts? And what of the offspring produced by this "marriage of convenience"?

Before and after he assumed power in 1922, Mussolini had frequently boasted of being a nonbeliever; in fact, no one who knew him had ever known him to attend mass. Realizing, however, that Church support was indispensable to his plans, he sought to cater to the clergy. Among other things, he brought the crucifix back into the classrooms of Italy, abolished Freemasonry, and granted churches substantial amounts of money to repair the buildings damaged during World War I. Il Duce even went so far as to go through a belated religious marriage to his wife and to have his growing children baptized in the Catholic rites. In time, the man who had once written a pamphlet entitled *God Does Not Exist,* and who had freely blasphemed and frequently attacked the Church, sometimes, through propaganda, attempted to palm himself off as a practicing Catholic and a professed believer. Very few people ever questioned him about his change of heart. Members of the clergy were particularly silent on the subject, for the clergy more than welcomed his stentorian support.

Because he needed help in entrenching himself as a political power, and wanted to improve his public image both in Italy and abroad, Mussolini paved the way for the settlement of the Vatican's long-standing grievance against the Italian state. The so-called Papal States lost during the Risorgimento had covered an area of some seventeen thousand square miles, including all of the city of Rome and a large hunk of territory north of the Eternal City and south of the River Po. The papal lands extended from the Tyrrhenian Sea to the Adriatic and included more than three million people. Although the popes had been hostile to the Risorgimento, by 1929 the Vatican was willing to accept a settlement for the loss of its temporal powers. When the Duce offered to make a deal, Pope Pius XI acceded.

It was raining heavily when Pietro Cardinal Gasparri drove into the Piazza Laterana on February 11, 1929, the day the agreement was to be signed. The noontime bells of the churches rang out, and Mussolini and his aides entered the Lateran Palace, to be greeted by Pope Pius' representatives. The signing was to take place in the same room in which Charlemagne had been the guest of Leo III over a thousand years earlier. Atop the long table—a gift of the Philippine Islands—were the inkwells, the blotters, the papers.

Nodding to the Duce as he entered the room, Cardinal Gasparri said, "I am happy to welcome you to our parochial house, and I rejoice that the treaties are being signed on the feast day of Notre Dame de Lourdes."

Mussolini registered no sign of recognition at this remark; the Cardinal then added, "And on the seventh anniversary of the coronation of His Holiness."

"Oh yes!" Mussolini said suddenly. "That particular coincidence has not escaped me!"

In silence the dictator went to the table and sat down

alongside the Cardinal. Pius had sent a gold pen, blessed by him, and after the Duce had affixed his signature and all the documents had been exchanged, Gasparri presented him the pen as a gift from the Pope. The two men shook hands and left the room. The whole affair had lasted less than thirty minutes.

When the news of the Church-State treaty was finally announced, the local citizenry—as well as the rest of the world—was startled. The Italian public, clearly pleased, accorded Benito Mussolini an overflow of support, which he himself had not perhaps anticipated. He became an idol to Catholic Italy. In thousands of homes, people cut pictures of the Duce from magazines and newspapers and pasted them on kitchen and living room walls. Youths splashed pro-Duce slogans in white paint on any flat surface available. Shovels he had used to inaugurate public projects were prized as relics. Wine glasses from which he had sipped were lovingly placed on shelves by restaurant owners. Young women by the thousands offered their favors to his virility—and let it be said that many of them, in fact, were ushered into the Duce's chambers.

But if the Lateran Treaty was a major coup for Mussolini, it was to be an even bigger victory for the Vatican. Mussolini, like all his bloodstained predecessors, has gone the way of all flesh, but the Vatican remains. And today the Vatican is solidly entrenched in the Italian economy.

The 1929 treaty was actually a unity of three separate agreements: the Lateran Pact, which provided for the creation of the new State of Vatican City; the Financial Convention, which granted payments to the Church for the loss of its temporal powers; and the Concordat, which gave the Vatican powers and privileges to administer its own special affairs.

According to the articles of the Lateran Pact, the State of Vatican City was set up as a sovereign entity. Three basilicas—San Giovanni Laterano, Santa Maria Maggiore, and San Paolo—and their accompanying buildings were classified as extraterritorial and were given immunity from Italian property taxes and real estate laws; the same status and immunity were given to the pontifical villa at Castel Gandolfo, where popes have traditionally spent their summer months, and also to a number of Church-owned office buildings in various parts of Rome. The Vatican agreed to recognize the existence of Italy and Italy's occupation of Rome as a permanent thing. And Italy agreed to accept the Church's canon law, which meant that divorces could not be granted by the state and that marriage ceremonies performed in church would fulfill civil requirements.

Under the terms of the Financial Convention, Italy consented to make a large money settlement for the loss of Vatican properties. A sum of $40 million was paid in one lump; in addition, 5 percent government bonds worth about $50 million were transferred to the Holy See. Italy also agreed to pay the salaries of parish priests stationed on its soil. (During the summer of 1959, the Italian parliament passed a law revising the pay scale provided for by this original agreement. Priests now receive $529 a year from the Italian government; higher-ranking clerics get about $600. Over thirty thousand priests are currently on the Italian payroll, a fact not generally known, even to the Italian people.)

The third document of the Lateran Treaty, the Concordat, carried a number of economic clauses that were of special interest to the Vatican. Members of the Roman Catholic clergy and citizens of the State of Vatican City were exempted from paying Italian taxes. The Church was given control of the various organizations, lay and clerical, functioning in the name of Catholicism throughout Italy. This meant that the Vatican would supervise the financial affairs of these organizations, which were referred to and defined as "ecclesiastical corporations." It also meant that the Italian government would have no legal right to intervene in activities of these organizations and could not block the formation of any new organization to which a pope granted approval.

The Concordat also stipulated that Protestant Bibles could no longer be distributed in Italy, that evangelical meetings in private homes were forbidden, and that Catholicism was to be Italy's official religion. Furthermore, religious teaching was to be extended into state schools and religion made a compulsory subject at the primary and secondary levels; Church-related educational institutions were to receive preferences over similar lay or state institutions. Finally, February 11 was named a national holiday to commemorate the signing of the treaty.

The noneconomic consequences the Lateran Treaty was to have in Italy need not concern us here. The financial effects of the pact were far reaching, however, though not immediately visible. On June 7, the very day the Lateran Treaty was ratified, Pope Pius created the Holy See's Special Administration and appointed Bernardino Nogara, a relative of the Archbishop of Udine, to watch over the large sum of money the Italian government had granted the Vatican. From the time Nogara received his appointment the names of prominent and trusted Vatican laymen began to appear on the boards of directors of various Italian companies. Significantly, Nogara's name rarely if ever showed on any company's roster of officers, but it is known that no Vatican layman, no matter how good his rapport with the pontifical family, could receive such an appointment if he did not have the blessing of Nogara. It should be mentioned that in later years the Nogara name did appear on a few corporation listings, where it was teamed in each case with several other key Vatican names.

What can be deduced from this is that Nogara wanted his own men in at the policy-making level of any company in which he placed Vatican funds. He made his careful investments one by one, and he appointed an "agent" to go with each. Where the sum was big, so was the name. Where the sum was bigger, several Vatican names could be found. Nogara never put "his" money into anything unless the sentinel went along.

One of Nogara's early targets was a gas combine called Italgas. Soon after the end of World War I, an Italian financier by the name of Rinaldo Panzarasa managed to get control of six small gas companies. These were La Stige, Italgas, La Società Italiana Industria Gas di Torino, La Gas e Coke di Milano, La Veneta Industria Gas di Venezia, and La Romana Gas; they furnished home fuel for twelve of Italy's largest cities, including Milan, Rome, Turin, and Venice. The companies were grouped by Panzarasa into a combine that came to be known as Italgas —and didn't prosper. In fact, Panzarasa's gas fortunes, figuratively, exploded.

By 1932, the worth of Panzarasa's group of companies had plunged from $13.7 million to $1.4 million. Italgas

69

was in trouble, and when the Fascist Italian government refused Panzarasa any kind of financial help, Nogara moved in swiftly. With Senator Alfredo Frassati and the Marquis Francesco Pacelli (whose brother later became Pope Pius XII) providing the front, Italgas fell into the embrace of the Vatican. Nogara built up this decadent organization so that it could begin to service other major cities in Italy. Today Italgas, which sold a total of 679 million cubic meters of gas during the fiscal year 1967–8, is the sole supplier of gas for Italian homes in thirty-six cities. The Vatican remains its controlling stockholder.

But all was not clear sailing after the Vatican embarked for new financial horizons. Italy, like other parts of the world, was lashed by economic storms between 1929 and 1933. Three of the country's major banks in which the Vatican had invested heavily—the Banco di Roma, the Banco di Santo Spirito, and the Sardinian Land Credit —were floundering. Among other problems, the largest of these banks, the Banco di Roma, possessed large packets of securities that had lost much of their worth and nearly all of their prestige. No one knows, even to this day, what deal Nogara made with Mussolini to bail out the Vatican, but in short order the moribund shares were transferred to the government holding company, I.R.I. (Istituto di Ricostruzione Industriale), that the Duce had formed as a catchall for shaky industrial organizations and banks. Mussolini, whose ignorance of economics made him an easy target for Nogara, let the Vatican bank transfer the securities, not for the current market prices, but for prices commensurate with their original worth. All told, I.R.I. paid the bank approximately $632 million—a sum far in excess of what the securities were then worth. The tremendous loss was written off by the Italian treasury.

Between 1929 and the outbreak of World War II, Nogara assigned Vatican capital and Vatican agents to work in diversified areas of Italy's economy—particularly in electric power, telephone communications, credit and banking, small railroads, and the production of agricultural implements, cement, and artificial textile fibers. Many of these ventures paid off.

Nogara gobbled up a number of companies including La Società Italiana della Viscosa, La Supertessile, La Società Meridionale Industrie Tessili, and La Cisaraion. Fusing these into one company, which he named CISA-Viscosa and placed under the command of Baron Francesco Maria Oddasso, one of the most highly trusted Vatican laymen, Nogara then maneuvered the absorption of the new company by Italy's largest textile manufacturer, SNIA-Viscosa. Eventually the Vatican interest in SNIA-Viscosa grew larger and larger, and in time the Vatican took control—as witness the fact that Baron Oddasso subsequently became vice president.

Thus did Nogara penetrate the textile industry. He penetrated other industries in other ways, for Nogara had many tricks up his sleeve. This selfless man, who probably did more to infuse life into the Italian economy than did any other single businessman in Italy's history, recognized that the subsurface strength of the Lateran Treaty lay in Clauses 29, 30, and 31 of the Concordat. Although some intellectuals had inveighed against the concessions Italy had made on education, marriage, and divorce, few observers had paid any close attention to those clauses of the Lateran Treaty that were mainly economic in nature. To most people they seemed of secondary importance.

But not to Nogara, the man with the dollar sign on his mind and the sign of the Cross in his heart. Clauses 29, 30, and 31 dealt with tax exemptions and the formation of new, tax-exempt "ecclesiastical corporations," over which the Italian state would have no controls.

Nogara reasoned that if he could get Mussolini to put a liberal interpretation on the word "ecclesiastical," he would be able to save Vatican corporations millions of dollars a year in Italian taxes. This was no small task, yet the Vatican Hercules succeeded at it.

The cunning Nogara euchred Mussolini into granting every Catholic corporation, whether its actual function was ecclesiastical or fiscal, either full exemption from taxes or substantial tax abatements. Somehow, Mussolini was convinced that a Vatican-owned bank was "a temple doing the work of God"! and that what was good for God was good for the Vatican—and that that was good for Italy.

The friendship of the Vatican and the Fascists continued throughout most of the thirties. It was especially strong after Italy invaded Ethiopia in 1935. A Nogara munitions plant supplied arms for the Italian army. But the friendship started to wane toward the end of the reign of Pius XI, who died in 1939.

When Pius XII took possession of the pontifical throne, Mussolini, who was suspicious of his polyglot intellectualism and believed him to possess the "evil eye," refused to kneel and kiss his hand, and he commanded photographers not to take pictures of him and Pius XII which would in any way convey the idea the Duce might be the humble servant of the Church. Relations between the Italian dictator and the Vatican had crumbled, but by then the Catholic Church was well entrenched in the Italian economy. Nogara was still steering the financial ship, and the Church had no worries about its future course.

Benito Mussolini had never quite been able to achieve the empire of which he dreamed, but he enabled the Vatican and Bernardino Nogara to create a dominion of another kind.

What
Is the
Pope?
VI

ONCE, DURING A solemn and symbolic ceremony in St. Peter's Basilica, when knickered throne-bearers were carrying Pope Pius XII down the center aisle, a little Italian boy of about twelve cried out to the pontiff in a voice plain to hear, "Santo Padre, I want to be like you someday—I want to be pope!"

His Holiness smiled at the lad and, as the dais-bearing porters paused for a moment, made a sign of the Cross, bent forward in his ornamented chair, and was overheard to say in whispered tones, "My son, being a pope isn't as great as you think."

Still awed by the sight of the pontiff's tall tiara and white-and-gold robe, the boy shrugged his shoulders in reverent resignation and said, "Then I don't want to be the pope either."

It might be appropriate here to examine the office of the papacy from a new angle. Theologians delve deeply into such questions as, Why is the Pope? and, Who is the Pope? Newspaper correspondents in Rome file thousands of words of copy each year on, Where is the Pope? and

How is the Pope? Few writers, however, deal with what may be the most significant question of all, What is the Pope?

At first this may not seem like a proper question, and yet the answer provides insight into the workings of the least populated state in the world, whose leader rules over the largest number of organized people in the world—some 550 million Roman Catholics. Since the 322 million Mohammedans, the 309 million Hindus, the 300 million Confucians, and the 202 million Protestants have never been able to overtake the Catholics in terms of numbers, the Vatican chief executive is the spiritual leader of the largest religious group on our planet.

The papal office is not without its impressive array of titles, official and unofficial. Officially the Pope is the Bishop of Rome, Successor of the Prince of Apostles, Supreme Pontiff of the Universal Church, Servant of the Servants of God, Patriarch of the West, Primate of Italy, Archbishop and Metropolitan of the Roman Province, and Sovereign of the State of Vatican City. Unofficially he is often called Rector of the World upon Earth, Father of Princes and Kings, Supreme Pontiff, and Pontifex Maximus. This last name is usually seen in abbreviated form, as "Pont.Max." (with no separation at the middle period). The Latin word *pontifex* means builder of bridges, and in ancient Rome the title Pontifex Maximus was given to the luminary who presided when a bridge was erected across the Tiber and the spirits of the river had to be conciliated. At the time of his murder, Julius Caesar was the Pontifex Maximus, but in the year 440 the title was transferred to Pope Leo I, and it has since unofficially remained with the papacy. Although no inscription on a fountain, building, or tomb in Rome seems complete unless a "Pont.Max." is included, no pope has personally used the signature for centuries. From the time of Gregory the Great, who died in the year 604, the title employed on papal bulls has been *Servus Servorum Dei,* Servant of the Servants of God.

The Vatican Archives contain a copy of a papal letter, an answer to one from Queen Victoria, indicating what one pontiff thought of his various designations. Queen Victoria, who apparently did not want to give acknowledgment to any of the papal titles, began her letter (which is also in the Vatican Archives) with "Most Eminent Sir" instead of the usual "Your Holiness." The pontiff was apparently offended. In his reply, he addressed Victoria as "The Most Serene and Powerful Victoria, Queen of the United Kingdom of Great Britain and Ireland and Other Regions, Illustrious Empress of India."

In Italy, the pope is generally called *Il Papa,* a title that comes from *pater patrum,* a Latin phrase meaning father of fathers. He is also referred to, most commonly in Rome, by the family name he gave up when elected. Thus the Romans call Pope Paul VI Papa Montini, just as they called Pope John XXIII Papa Roncalli, and Pius XII Papa Pacelli. To some people, the use of the last name may seem disrespectful or irreverent. It isn't, however. For one thing, the Italians are accustomed to having the pope in their midst. He may be idolized, worshiped, and esteemed by pious Italians, but he is often taken for granted in Rome and is regarded in other parts of Italy more as a man than as a saintly being.

Without meaning any insult whatever, the Italians tell many jokes about the papacy. One especially good anecdote made the rounds when Clare Booth Luce was the

United States ambassador to Italy (*l'ambassatrice,* the Italians called her).

Converts, say the Italians, are the most fervent of Catholics. The story is about the time Mrs. Luce, a convert, was received in private audience by Pope Pius XII. Neither she nor the Pope emerged from the reception chamber for a long, long time. Vatican aides began to fret. After several hours they peeked into the room. The Pope was backed up into a corner; Mrs. Luce, talking a blue streak, paused for breath. "But, Mrs. Luce," the aides heard the Pope say in a gentle, yet quivering voice, "I already *am* a Roman Catholic!"

Another story, told by Bill Pepper, *Newsweek*'s former resident correspondent in Rome, is perhaps closer to the truth. It concerns the first time Pope John's relatives visited the Apostolic Palace after his coronation. An impressive experience for anyone, a papal audience can evoke in a devout person a tremendous sense of humility. On the occasion of the special audience for John's family, the relatives walked timidly through the golden halls, past the omnipresent Swiss Guards. When they saw John, dressed in his pontifical white robes, they dropped to their knees and bowed their heads.

"*Lasciate perdere* (Forget all that)!" said John. "Don't be afraid. It's only me!"

When a man is elected pope, he loses many things. He loses his family name. He loses most of the civil ties that bind him to the country of his birth. Moreover, a new pope finds that his daily life is regulated, often down to the most minute detail, by tradition. The men around him may change, but those who replace them have the same functions to carry out, according to the same well-imbedded customs.

77

The pope's confessor, an ordinary priest, must be a Jesuit; he must visit the Vatican once a week at a fixed time, and he alone may absolve the pope of his sins. The master of the Apostolic Palace must be a Dominican; the sacristan an Augustinian. If a pope changed any of this, a whole religious order would regard the gesture as an affront.

Newly elected popes have reacted in many ways when they realized they had become the Supreme Pontiff of the Universal Church. Pius X, a simple man, was at first terrified to find himself a monarch who is a slave to his mission. Pointing at the Swiss Guards standing sentry outside his apartment, he once whispered to an old friend, "There are my jailers!"

One of former New York *Herald Tribune* Rome correspondent Barrett McGurn's favorite stories has to do with the time Pius XII was readying a speech for the occasion of an English Catholic centennial.

"How do you pronounce 'centenary'?" he asked an American prelate.

"SEN-tenerry," answered the Yank, putting the accent on the first syllable.

"But don't the British say sin-TEE-nerry?" the pontiff asked.

"Yes, Your Holiness—but four fifths of the English-speaking world speak in American style."

"But it's the English language—the British started it. It's for them to say how it should be used."

"Sin-TEE-nerry," with the accented second syllable, was the way the Pope pronounced it during his discourse a few days later. Nevertheless, when an English bishop paid a visit some time after that, Pius made haste to ask him, "How do you pronounce 'centenary'?" For the rest

78

of his life the polyglot Pope kept seeking opinions on that one word.

The pope, being one of the world's few absolute rulers, is not easy to speak with—yet he is the easiest chief of state to see. Most popes hold frequent audiences in the Apostolic Palace (Paul VI's audiences are often on Wednesdays at noon). On Sundays, usually at noon, popes customarily appear at the window of the top-floor papal apartment to bless the crowds standing in St. Peter's Square. Pope John emerged many times from his sheltered quarters to make visits in Rome and in other parts of Italy. Paul VI has visited more countries (India, the Middle Eastern countries, the United States, Portugal, Turkey, Colombia) than any other pope in history—and each time his presence has attracted huge crowds of Catholics and non-Catholics alike.

There is no question of the pope's charismatic appeal. Despite the fact that there are millions of people who owe the pope no spiritual allegiance, papal influence in world affairs has compelled nations and their leaders to extend the pope diplomatic courtesies normally reserved for civil rulers. No other religious leader in the world is afforded such treatment. No single state officer has been such a consistent drawing card, away from his immediate domain, as has the man who sits on Peter's Chair in the Eternal City.

Avro Manhattan, a frequent commentator on Vatican affairs, attributes much of the papal lure to the dual nature of the Church. He once told me in a taped interview, "Although the most uniform of religious institutions, the Church is also the most diversified. While the most unchangeable, she has a genius for adaptability; and while constantly obsessed with things pertaining to a future life,

79

she is vigorously active in controlling things pertaining to this world. Last but not least, she has the greatest centralization of power in the world.

"Her administration," Manhattan continued, "is unique. Although a church, she is at the same time a sovereign government. Although a mighty religious institution, she is also a mighty political presence and a major economic center. Although her officials are drawn from many nationalities, when acting as members of her government they have none; while speaking the major languages of the world, she issues her ordinances in one which only a few can understand. Although territorially the smallest state in existence, hers is the most significant in the world. And although neither an empire, a kingdom, nor a republic, it is a mixture of all three.

"The head of such government wears not one but three crowns. Although without an army, a navy, or hydrogen bombs, he has more power than if he had at his disposal the greatest arsenal on the globe. Spiritually and hierarchically, no one is above him except God, the source of his authority."

Once again we come, then, to the question, What is the Pope? This can be answered or explained in part by reviewing the duties, responsibilities, powers, and operations of the papacy.

Lord paramount of the Holy See, the pope is first among his bishops, all of whom come under his direct jurisdiction; in theory he has full and absolute power over the Roman Catholic Church. Every decree requires his approval. He can obey or ignore precedent. He can set aside tradition; he can write (or rewrite) constitutions; he can change discipline without consultation; he can proclaim dogmas on his own. Although on important matters the pope is supposed to seek counsel and advice from the College of Cardinals, he is empowered to make up his own mind and take action. On theological questions, the pope invariably consults with his bishops and cardinals, but, on matters of high policy, he may evolve a course of action without any previous consultations, as did Pope John when, without calling in the Curia cardinals for their views, he decided to go ahead with the Ecumenical Council.

The pope has executive as well as legislative and judiciary powers. He can be judged by no man, and there is no appeal from his decisions. In this respect his position is tantamount to that of a sovereign who cannot be brought to court. Acting in his executive capacity, the pope may (1) approve or sanction or suppress religious orders, (2) grant indulgences, (3) beatify or canonize saints, (4) appoint bishops, (5) erect, administer, alter, or suppress bishoprics, (6) assign an auxiliary bishop to one who is incapacitated, (7) found and legislate for papal universities, (8) issue liturgical books, (9) administer the temporal goods of ecclesiastical foundations, (10) erect and govern missions dependent on the Holy See.

As a legislator, the pope may (1) call, preside over, and adjourn ecumenical councils, (2) regulate holy days and Catholic feasts, (3) introduce new rites and abrogate old ones, (4) issue ex cathedra decretals on belief, (5) introduce, alter, or suppress Church laws on any subject, (6) defend doctrine against heresies, (7) define fast days and periods of fasting.

Also liberally defined are the pope's judicial duties. He may (1) relax vows and oaths for members of the religious who want to return to secular life, (2) give matrimonial dispensations, (3) act as a court, (4) establish rules of judicial procedure, (5) establish censures or punishments, (6) organize courts for hearing cases, (7) organize courts or appoint synodal judges for the diocese of Rome.

Inasmuch as the men elected to the papacy tend to be advanced in years, there is always the question of whether a septuagenarian or an octogenarian could become mentally enfeebled while serving as pontiff. Rome correspondent Robert Neville once took this problem to a Vatican prelate and asked him what would happen if a pope were to lose his reason or become physically incapacitated. Neville pointed out that the fact that popes are elected for life, with no provisions either for their recall or for their abdication, and the further facts that there is no proviso in Church regulations for creating a regency and that the College of Cardinals cannot be legally convened to take over made the problem appear insoluble.

The Vatican officer said, "The Good Lord seems to protect the Church from such a catastrophe. Popes just apparently do not lose their mind or reason. But should the impossible happen, I believe the Vatican bureaucracy would act as an effective brake against rash or embarrassing acts."

To better understand the question, What is the Pope? one must examine the structure of the Holy See, which is the government of the Vatican and of the Roman Catholic Church.

As the head of his church, the pope runs a vast business. He runs it as a corporate structure, working with twelve congregations (committees) of cardinals—a system that dates from the late sixteenth century—and with three apostolic tribunals and five departmental offices. Because he is the chief executive officer of the State of Vatican City, the pope is guaranteed independence of any civil power. No other religious leader in the world enjoys a comparable position.

To understand the foundations of papal authority is to understand who, why, and what a pope is. His primacy of jurisdiction, not only over the clerics but also over the hundreds of millions of the faithful, extends to matters affecting his religion, but it also extends to all other matters in which the Roman Catholic Church is interested throughout the world. Using his wide religious authority, the pope plays a distinctive role in the affairs of the world, exercising a power that is independent of his temporal position as head of Vatican City. The 550 million people who are Roman Catholics are but a modest number of the hundreds of millions who recognize the juridical sovereignty of the Holy See as a moral authority while not agreeing in substance with Catholicism's theological basis.

Various countries of the world therefore maintain diplomatic relations with the Vatican. Papal ambassadors are to be found not only in Catholic nations but also in Protestant, Islamic, Buddhist, and atheist countries. An ambassador of the pope is called a nuncio, and he has the same status as the ambassador of any great power. At this writing, while Pope Paul is still reigning, the Vatican maintains official ambassadors in the following countries: Argentina, Austria, Belgium, Bolivia, Brazil, Burundi, Cameroon, Chile, China (Taiwan), Colombia, the Congo (Leopoldville), Costa Rica, Cuba, Czechoslovakia, the Dominican Republic, Ecuador, Egypt, El Salvador, Estonia, Ethiopia, Finland, France, Germany,

Guatemala, Haiti, Honduras, Hungary, India, Indonesia, Iran, Iraq, Ireland, Italy, Japan, Kenya, Korea (Seoul), Latvia, Lebanon, Liberia, Lithuania, Luxembourg, Malawi, Malta, the Netherlands, Nicaragua, Pakistan, Panama, Paraguay, Peru, the Philippines, Poland, Portugal, Rumania, Rwanda, Senegal, Spain, Switzerland, Syria, Turkey, Uruguay, Venezuela, Yugoslavia, Zambia.

If a country does not have a nuncio, the Vatican bypasses the problem by nominating a representative without the official status of an ambassador; such representatives are called apostolic delegates. Officially an envoy of the pope, the apostolic delegate is unofficially an ambassador in the guise of an ecclesiastical official of the Catholic Church. He is not accredited by the government of the country in which he stays, but in practice he is usually given many of the courtesies and privileges extended to fully recognized ambassadors. At present, the following countries give hospitality to apostolic delegates: Albania, Australia, Bulgaria, Cambodia, Canada, Great Britain, Greece, Laos, Mexico, New Zealand, Tanzania, Thailand, the United States, and Vietnam (Saigon). Apostolic delegates are also maintained in Copenhagen for the Scandinavian countries, in Algiers for North Africa, in Nairobi for East Africa, in Dakar for West Africa, in Pretoria for South Africa, in Lagos for Central West Africa, and in Yaounde for Central Africa.

Adjudged by the bar of world opinion and international law, the pope enjoys immunity from the territorial jurisdiction of any human authority. Consider what happened when Hitler's occupation troops in Rome completely surrounded the pope's tiny state. German soldiers never crossed the frontier. Had they decided to invade

Vatican City, the blitzkrieg would have taken all of a half hour, and the man who was then pope would have been conquered—but not defeated. In his own way, Hitler provided a dramatic confirmation of the real, if intangible, moral authority of the pope, however diminutive his territory. The pontiff's unique position in the world was aptly expressed by one writer, who said, "The pope is not sovereign because he is the ruler of the Vatican state; he is the ruler of the Vatican because he is a sovereign."

The papal case is, of course, unique in contemporary international law and diplomatic practice. It is said that Winston Churchill, during a visit with Joseph Stalin, attempted to convince the Soviet dictator of the advisability of having the Vatican as an ally. Stalin, the story goes, asked derisively, "How many divisions does the Pope have?"

According to one reporter, the episode was related to Pope Pius, who commented, "Mr. Stalin will meet my legions in the other world!"

Of the pontiff's celestial consociates little can be said here. In the practical day-to-day world of the twentieth century, His Holiness often depends on terrestrial colleagues to help him carry out his complex operations. The pope has under him the Roman Curia—the body of congregations, tribunals, and departmental offices. The congregations, corresponding somewhat to the ministries of other countries, include the Sacred Congregation for the Doctrine of the Faith (which before the recent Curia reforms was the Holy Office), the Congregation for Bishops (formerly the Consistorial Congregation), the Congregation for the Oriental Churches, the Congregation for the Discipline of Sacraments, the Congregation for the Clergy (formerly the Congregation of the Council), the Congregation for the Religious and for Secular Institutes (formerly the Congregation for the Religious), the Congregation for the Propagation of the Faith (which is now also called the Congregation for the Evangelization of the Nations), the Congregation of Rites, and the Congregation for Catholic Education (formerly the Congregation of Seminaries and Universities). Though these overlap a bit, the cardinals who serve in the Curia are formed into one of two "parties," which comprise the conservative and the progressive elements. These "parties" can exercise pressure on given papal decisions—such as the bitter pill Paul was made to swallow with the recent encyclical against birth control.

Next to the pope himself, the single most important individual in the Vatican hierarchy is his immediate aide, the secretary of state—whose duties correspond to those of the prime minister in other government organizations. For most of his tenure in office (1939–1958), Pope Pius kept the post in his own hands. But this is not usually the case. Most popes have leaned heavily on the secretary of state—Pope John once described a secretary of state as "my closest collaborator"—because the secretary's office has a variety of major functions. The secretary recommends to the pontiff the names of men to represent the Vatican abroad, has jurisdiction over all such appointees, gives instructions to Catholic lay organizations all over the world (thus often exerting pressure on the internal affairs of foreign countries), prepares the texts of agreements with foreign countries, participates in the appointment of bishops, confers Vatican honors and titles, and deals with such ecclesiastical questions as divorce and contraception. Often the secretary of state represents His Holiness at official ceremonies. The secretary sits on the pontifical committee for the government of Vatican City, and he serves as the Vatican's chief negotiator. One of his most important duties is that of overseeing the cardinals' committee on the finances of the Vatican.

Veritably the most active officer now in the Vatican, the present secretary of state is the only person who sees Pope Paul on matters of business at least once a day; often he communicates with his immediate superior over the phone as many as a dozen times in one morning. One of his duties is to prepare a daily summary of world press reports for the papal desk. Vatican authorities are inclined to believe the Pope is one of the best-informed chiefs of state in the world—better, they assert, than the President of the United States.

News of all kinds—ecclesiastical, political, economic —comes to the Vatican through a gigantic machine that extends to the remotest corners of the earth. Nuncios and apostolic delegates, who have access to the same information ambassadors and representatives of other governments do, send frequent reports to the secretary of state. But by far the most elaborate reports come from the bishops. Nearly fifteen hundred bishops, scattered all over the globe, send in periodic accounts on matters of interest to the Holy See. Consequently, an enormous amount of correspondence reaches the Vatican every day, including up-to-the-minute stock market analyses and incisive views of current economic trends.

In addition to this "espionage" service, the Vatican requires that each bishop come to Rome to see the Pope personally at least once every five years if he is stationed in Europe, and once every ten years if he is stationed elsewhere. On his arrival, the visitor must submit a report on his diocese; the report must answer a specific set of questions, which covers spiritual, ecclesiastical, social, physical, and economic conditions among the clergy and the parishioners. Considered extraordinarily accurate, these reports go deeply into the sentiments and feelings of the populace of the countries or regions concerned. Any bishop—or for that matter, any clergyman of any rank—who has a report of an urgent nature can communicate in code with the Vatican's secretary of state by cable or by radio. The secretary of state will quickly pass the message to His Holiness if he considers the dispatch of top priority.

One of the most efficient secretaries of state in recent years was Pope John's first secretary, Domenico Cardinal Tardini. The two men had excellent rapport with each other, but the Cardinal also had his differences with John —a fact that was often bandied about in inner Vatican circles. A stubborn Roman who could not fathom John's desire to "open up" the Church to the outside world, Cardinal Tardini was bothered by his superior's "new ways." Tardini, whose office was one floor below the Pope's, had a habit, especially when miffed, of referring to John as "the one up there." Since news tidbits and gossip travel quickly inside the Vatican, it wasn't long before word got to John, who summoned Tardini forthwith.

"I'd like to clear up a matter," the Pope said. " 'The one up there' is the Lord, the Eternal Father in Heaven. I'm just 'the one on the fourth floor.' So I beg of you, don't throw confusion into the ranks."

Building a
Business by
Building Buildings
VII

PERCHED ATOP Monte Mario and overlooking a panorama of ancient ruins and Renaissance settings is the busiest of Rome's new international hotels, the one flying the Hilton flag. Of the thousands of persons who use the four hundred rooms and suites in the Cavalieri Hilton each year, few are aware that the hotel is largely owned by the Catholic Church. Through the Società Generale Immobiliare, the Vatican has a big interest in the hilltop hotel, which is operated by Hilton International. Said interest is, to be exact, a three-quarter ownership.

As the largest of Italy's construction companies, the Vatican-owned Società Generale Immobiliare has been in business for more than a century. S.G.I. has entered every facet of the building business—not only construction but also planning, investment, production of specialized building materials and equipment, and management.

From 1870, when S.G.I., Italy's oldest construction company, moved its headquarters from Turin to Rome, until the end of World War II, S.G.I.'s interests and properties were concentrated in and around the Eternal City. Then the company branched out on a nationwide scale, growing into a diversified corporation which took on thousands of new employees. Now S.G.I. has moved onto the international scene. It has thrust itself into the business of constructing large-scale residential projects and selling them to private customers. And lately, this Vatican company has become involved in urban development, with the planning and building of entire metropolitan or suburban centers and communities.

S.G.I.'s investment in construction projects has jumped to over $45 million at this writing. Its gross assets, which were approximately $50 million in 1955, were about $170 million in 1967, while net earnings went from $2.4 million in 1955 to $6.2 million in 1967. Today S.G.I. holds a controlling or substantial interest in over fifty Italian companies. Four of these specialize in investment and property holdings; nineteen are real estate development institutions; nine deal with urban development projects; four engage in agricultural works; eight are industrial and manufacturing corporations; and the rest are technical and service companies.

Although Italy's housing industry recently suffered a serious slump, S.G.I. was not badly hurt. Its earnings still rose 16 percent and its gross assets went up 20 percent. Moreover, the Vatican company's investment in land increased 25 percent, due largely to the completion of a long-term plan that involved the formation of a satellite city near Milan.

Nevertheless, there was a slowdown in the sales of S.G.I.'s newly finished buildings. Against a background of reduced mortgage credit facilities, Vatican strategy called for a corresponding increase in S.G.I.'s bank borrowing (from a Vatican bank, to be sure). A satisfactory ratio between current assets and liabilities was restored following the successful issue of 6 percent convertible debentures for the equivalent of $26 million.

In 1966, in Rome alone, the Vatican's construction society completed or nearly completed three apartment houses, seven garden villages, twelve luxury homes, a five-building apartment development, an office building with ground-floor stores and a cellar garage, two other office buildings (comprising 174 office units), and a twelve-villa garden development.

During the same year, in Milan, S.G.I. finished a three-building housing project that has sixty-two family dwellings, eighteen offices, seventeen stores, and an eighty-car garage. Plans have been drawn to add two more buildings to the project by replacing the old Vatican-owned structures on an adjoining site. Elsewhere in Milan, and also in 1966, S.G.I. completed a seven-building (196-apartment) housing complex and was in the process of putting up a shopping center. The shopping center's site is the famed Piazza Loreto, the square where the bullet-riddled bodies of Mussolini and his girl friend were hanged upside down during the closing days of the war.

In Genoa, 1966, S.G.I. nearly finished a 150-apartment development along the Via Bobbio, opened and rented to capacity its plush Residence Park Riviera, and began construction of a new 92-apartment development. And plans were made by an affiliate of S.G.I. (the Eden di Nervi Company) to build a large motel just outside Genoa, in an area near the Vatican-owned Hotel Eden.

S.G.I., which recently moved from its cramped headquarters in downtown Rome to an eight-story glass building in the city's outskirts, has also put into execution building projects of various sorts in other parts of Italy. In Florence, Naples, Palermo, and Catania many of its undertakings are handled by related companies. Few people know which of the related companies belong to S.G.I. and which are controlled by parental pursestrings. S.G.I. guards her fifty plus offspring like a mother hen, preferring to shield them from too much attention. This is done for a number of reasons, some having to do with taxation and others with regional strategy.

To illustrate: S.G.I. does not own Rome's Cavalieri Hilton directly. The three-quarter owner is a front company called Italo Americana Nuovi Alberghi (I.A.N.A.), which answers only to S.G.I. Similarly, the Società Italiana Arredamenti Metallici (S.I.A.M.) is owned by the Vatican but administered indirectly by S.G.I. S.I.A.M., which runs a large plant for the production of steel furniture, was the company that supplied the steel furnishings for the Italian luxury liners the *Raffaello* and the *Michelangelo*.

S.G.I.'s other companies include the Compagnia Italiana degli Alberghi dei Cavalieri (C.I.D.A.L.C.), which operates hotels in Pisa and Milan; Bellrock Italiana and S.A.R.F.E.C., which produce specialized building materials; and the Manifattura Ceramica Pozzi, which manufactures petrochemicals, plastic products, and plumbing fixtures.

Italy has no regulations or laws against private holding companies, and S.G.I. controls several.

One of the largest is the Società Generale per Lavori e Pubbliche Utilità (S.O.G.E.N.E.), a construction company with extensive experience in public works. In recent years the Vatican-owned S.O.G.E.N.E. has built a 328-

foot-high dam at Mulargia in Sardinia, a 430,000-square-foot, reinforced concrete flood-water diversion for the Arno River at Pisa, a 125-foot dam at Gramolazzo near Lucca, a hydroelectric power plant near Terni, a 54-mile consortium aqueduct for the cities of Ascoli and Fermo, a 29,950-foot tunnel for the pipes of the projected Frida Aqueduct, hundreds of miles of embankments for Italy's main superhighway, the tunnel for the Gran San Bernardo highway connecting Italy to Switzerland, concrete emplacements for much of Milan's new subway, the 4.5-mile-long highway between Chiasso and San Gottardo, and a number of bridges and viaducts in various parts of the country.

Demonstrating a know-how that makes it far more than an ordinary general contractor, S.O.G.E.N.E. has even produced entire factories under private contract. The impressive new Colgate-Palmolive plant at Anzio, which covers 430,000 square feet of land and has over seventeen million cubic feet of interior space, was designed and put up by S.O.G.E.N.E. technicians and engineers—that is, by experts who drew their pay from Vatican coffers. This same team of experts also built the $565-million Italsider iron and steel complex; the largest such complex in all Europe, this one, in Taranto, sprawls over 3.9 million square feet of land. A telecommunications plant at San Siro was set up by S.O.G.E.N.E., which handled the entire project. In Sardinia the same Vatican contractors set up not long ago a 64,000-kilowatt thermoelectric power plant (near Cagliari) and a 480,000-kilowatt plant (at Sulcis). Working for Italy's nationalized electric industry (E.N.E.L.), busy S.O.G.E.N.E. teams installed a 200,000-kilowatt thermoelectric power structure at Civitavecchia and a 300,000-kilowatt plant near Perugia.

On opening day, all of S.O.G.E.N.E.'s projects are given the customary blessing by an attending cardinal, and often there is a special good luck message from the Pope himself. The sign of the Cross was made many times in 1966, when S.O.G.E.N.E. completed public and private works that totaled $27.6 million. Although this figure is 25 percent less than that for the preceding year, a decrease attributed to Italy's economic dip, the outlook for S.O.G.E.N.E. is good, for a number of public projects have already been contracted for and Italy's economic situation shows every sign of improving.

Most of S.G.I.'s enterprises outside of Italy have been undertaken by still another subsidiary company, Ediltecno, S.p.A. Fully owned by S.G.I., it was liquidated in 1967. Ediltecno, which was organized in 1961 to service projects abroad, was a technical, consulting, and engineering management company with branch offices in Washington and Paris and a representative in New York City. There is also a Canadian company known as Ediltecno (Canada) Limited, located in Montreal, and a Latin American affiliate called Ediltecno de Mexico, S.A., based in Mexico City.

In the past seven years S.G.I. has acquired a controlling interest—nearly 70 percent of the common stock and 50 percent of the preferred—in Watergate Improvements, Inc., of Washington, D.C. Through it, the Vatican is playing a major part in the completion of a large office-and-apartment complex on the edge of the Potomac. The first stage of the project was finished in 1965 with the completion of Watergate East, a thirteen-story cooperative apartment building with 238 apartments, 60,000 square feet of commercial space, and five acres of parking on four underground levels. During the project's second stage, completed in 1967, a thirteen-story apartment hotel with three underground levels, 221 suites, 10,000 square feet of commercial space, and a 40,000-square-foot indoor garage was built, as was an eleven-story office building with 180,000 square feet of office space. Work on the third stage began in 1967, and by 1969 a building of 144 apartments near Washington's Rock Creek Parkway is expected to be finished. Then the fourth and last stage of the project (the plans of which have not yet been made known) will begin. Altogether, the luxury project in the Foggy Bottom section of the U.S. capital is expected to cost in the vicinity of $65 million.

In Canada, S.G.I. is active through subsidiary companies. For instance, it is the largest single stockholder, owning 85 percent of the shares, in Montreal's Redbrooke Estates Limited. Redbrooke recently completed, in one of the most fashionable sections of Montreal, a thirty-three-story apartment building with three underground levels. Including 224 apartment units and 100,-000 square feet of indoor parking, the structure (known as Port-Royal) has been taken over by a newly formed Vatican company called Immobiliare-Canada Limited. The company has a capital (in Canadian dollars) of $456,900 and share obligations of $14.4 million, of which S.G.I. holds 93 percent. Immobiliare-Canada owns the forty-seven-story Montreal office building, the Stock Exchange Tower, that houses the Canadian and Montreal stock exchanges. The building cost approximately forty-seven million Canadian dollars and was designed with the cooperation of Rome's Pier Luigi Nervi, the cement wizard. Over 600 feet high, it is believed to be the tallest reinforced concrete building in the world. Another Vatican-controlled company in Canada is the Sogesan Construction Company Limited, which has been putting up one-family houses southwest of metropolitan Montreal. In the community known as Greendale, Sogesan has so far built and sold over three hundred houses and is still building and selling.

In Mexico, the Lomas Verdes S.A. de C.V. construction company is building a suburban city on some thirteen hundred acres of scenic land outside Mexico City, near Tlalnepantla; the city will ultimately house about a hundred thousand persons. S.G.I. owns about 30 percent of the Mexican company's stock and is providing the technical consultants and the project manager. A four-lane, tree-lined superhighway, La Superavenida, connecting the new city to the main superhighway and thus to the center of Mexico City, has already been completed by Lomas Verdes. Another Vatican-affiliated company, Immobiliaria Corinto S.A. (in which S.G.I. holds one-third interest) is engaged in building five sixteen-story apartment houses in Mexico City's fashionable Paseo de Las Palmas sector.

In France during 1967, the Vatican's S.I.C.E. company (Sociétè Immobilière Champs-Élysees), a French company with its head office in Paris, completed work on an elegant marble-faced office building on Paris' Avenue des Champs-Élysees. The nine-story structure, with four underground levels, provides 110,000 square feet of office space and 87,000 square feet of indoor parking.

With Vatican-owned construction companies building everywhere, there have inevitably been some hints of scandal. Not the least interesting of these stories, which are almost invariably suppressed by the Italian press, was that of the sale to the Italian government of church-owned real estate for the 1960 Olympic installations.

In 1958, shortly before Italy took on the responsibility of hosting the Olympics in Rome, the Vatican owned more than 102 million square feet of property within Rome's city limits. These holdings made it the biggest landowner, apart from the government, in all Italy. They were accumulated by the Vatican through quiet purchase, inheritances, donations, and foreclosures over a long period of time.

The National Italian Olympic Committee purchased large stretches of land from the Holy See for an unspecified sum and erected some fifteen stadiums at a cost of almost $29 million. To connect the sport structures located in the northern part of the city with those in the southern sector, Rome built the Olympic Highway. The throughway followed a circuitous route because it was placed on land that the city of Rome had purchased from front companies owned by the Società Generale Immobiliare.

Although the deals for this land had been made long before any mention of public bids, they might have passed unnoticed had it not been for the fact that the speedway began to sprout major cracks and crevices shortly after the Olympic athletes returned to their homelands. Società Generale Immobiliare, which had participated in the building of the road through several front companies, at that point offered to resurface the holes under a series of new contracts from the municipal government; the offer was accepted, for sums that were never disclosed, and the potholes and splits in the Olympic Highway were finally covered up. So was the scandal—almost.

There's No Business Like
Vatican Business
VIII

THE TALE OF the eel that one day left its home in Lake Bracciano, some fifty miles outside Rome, and swam all the way to Vatican City to make an unscheduled "appearance" underneath the Pope's window has every earmark of a fish story—and yet it happened.

The eel, in swimming around the bottom of the lake, apparently slithered into a cement water pipe. At a point forty-six miles from where the fish started, the main forked off in two directions—one way went to Rome, and the other to Vatican City. Bearing to the right, the eel took the way that led to the Vatican. After passing another underground junction, the eel slipped into a drain and managed to get itself stuck inside one of the two famed fountains in St. Peter's Square, just below the papal chambers.

The eel was blocking off the fountain's water. But the irreverent creature would not have made its mark on Vatican history if it hadn't been for Pope Pius XII, who had just finished shaving when he glanced out the window and noticed to his bewilderment that there was no water in the fountain. At breakfast he commented to his housekeeper on how odd it was that there was water gushing from the far fountain but not from "our fountain."

Sister Pasqualina picked up the phone and called the fire department. The firemen arrived, as did some newspapermen, and when the fountain's innards were examined, the eel was found. When it was removed from the tiny pipe in which it was lodged, the fountain came to life again. The eel was carried away in a pail.

A few days later, a newspaper reporter asked what had become of the eel. Since the Vatican ignores all such questions, cynical Romans provided their own answer. The Vatican, they claimed, had taken the eel to one of Rome's many outdoor fishmarkets, and sold it—which, they said, put the Pope in the fish business as well as every other.

What actually happened to the aquatic intruder is, of course, not known. But the story does indicate what Italian skeptics think about the Vatican and its business interests. According to these cynics, the Vatican is involved in so many business enterprises that even the selling of fish would not be beneath its dignity. As far as anyone knows for sure, the Vatican is not presently in competition with Rome's outdoor fishmongers. But many Romans are inclined to believe some of the Vatican's financial operations do have a fishy odor about them.

So widespread and complex are the Vatican's money-making enterprises, that it is almost impossible to get a clear picture of all of them.

In the last chapter we described Vatican participation in the building and construction industry through the Società Generale Immobiliare. In this chapter we will try to trace the Vatican's participation in manufacturing, energy, communications, banking, insurance, and other fields. The reader is asked to take a deep breath before entering the maze.

There is hardly a sector of Italy's economy in which the Vatican's "men of trust" are not representing the Church's interests. Almost all of these men hold high positions in companies in which the Church is financially involved. They hold their responsible posts year in and year out, sometimes on the basis of the percentage of profit that the Holy See realizes on its investment.

For many years, Bernardino Nogara served on the board of directors of the Montecatini Company (now Montecatini Edison). Let us take a look at this company. One of the largest corporations in Italy, and indeed, in the world, it deals in mining and metallurgical products, fertilizers, synthetic resins, textile fibers, and pharmaceuticals as well as electric power—and it is bound to the Vatican with hoops of steel. The extent of Vatican participation in this major corporation is not known; probably the Vatican does not have a majority holding, but its interest is substantial indeed. Since the death of Nogara, several Vatican watchdogs have replaced him on the company's board and take part in all the important decisions, such as that in 1966 to merge Montecatini and the Edison Company. For that year of the merger Montecatini Edison reported total sales of $683.9 million and a net profit of $62.6 million. The 1967 report and balance sheet showed substantial boosts in nearly all sectors of the company's activities, with total sales having jumped to $854 million and the net profit to $66.1 million. Montecatini's investments in other companies amount to over $942 million, its real estate holdings to better than $22 million, and its industrial plants to approximately $1.3 billion.

100

Montecatini Edison has a number of foreign associate companies, all of which are doing well. The Novamont Corporation at Neal, West Virginia, is doubling its production capacity to take advantage of the expanding polypropylene market in the United States. In Holland, the Compagnie Néerlandaise de L'Azote recently modernized its plant at Sluiskil and increased its daily production to one thousand tons of ammonia and two thousand tons of nitrogenous fertilizers; it also began construction of a new plant that will produce six hundred tons of urea a day. In Spain, Paular, S.A., in which Montecatini Edison has a joint holding, completed a new factory at Puertollano for the manufacture of polypropylene and polypropylene products. The Madras Aluminum Company of India expects to increase its production of alumina to fifty thousand tons a year and that of aluminum to twenty-five thousand tons a year. The continually expanding Brazilian Heliogas group recently acquired 140,000 new users and has increased its annual sales of liquid gas to about one hundred sixty thousand tons. And Panedile Argentina during 1967 brought its work on the damming of the Rio Hondo and the construction of a hydroelectric power station at Ullun to completion.

In Italy, Montecatini Edison owns or controls nineteen companies. These include Società Orobia, Mineraria Prealpina, Miniere di Ravi, Sorap-Società Raffinazione Petroli, Miana Serraglia, Ascona, Clio, Fortuna, Hermes, Immobiliare Capricorno, Melide, Parnaso, Ribolla, Sant-Agostino and Società Mineraria Presolana, all of Milan; and Cieli and Società Imprese Elettriche Scrivia, both of Genoa; Società Emiliana di Esercizi Elettrici of Parma; and Resia of Casoria.

Now in its second century of existence, Italcementi—which came under Vatican control after the war and is run by papal "agent" Carlo Pesenti—accounts for 32 percent of the total cement production of Italy; it is the world's fifth largest producer of cement and the second largest in Europe. In 1967, Italcementi, which employs over 6,500 workers, reported a net profit of $5.5 million, and it produced more than twenty-six million tons. The company, which has its headquarters in Bergamo, has a capital of $51.2 million. Because of a crisis in Italy's building industry in the last few years, Italcementi's profits had somewhat decreased (they were over $4.2 million in 1965, and not quite $4 million in 1966). The company had taken the decrease more or less in its stride, and according to Massimo Spada (speaking for the board of directors), expects to show up even stronger in 1969 and 1970 when construction picks up again. Thus, Italcementi recently built and put into operation a new cement plant near Brescia. The plant, which covers an area of over two million square feet, produces six hundred thousand tons of cement a year. Much of this is a new white cement known as Supercemento Italbianco which is quick drying and highly resistant to breakage.

The SNIA-Viscosa Company of Milan, which produces more than 70 percent of Italy's artificial and synthetic textile fibers, is known to be maneuvered by Vatican financiers. It is not owned by the Vatican. It is, however, tied to the CISA-Viscosa Company, which produces viscose fibers and rayon, and to the Saici Company, which manufactures cellulose—and both of these companies are owned by the Vatican. Also, SNIA-Viscosa holds considerable stock in a cotton plant, Cotonificio Veneziano, which is a Vatican-controlled company. SNIA-Viscosa, which has a capital of $89.6 million, has among its shareholders the British textile group Courtaulds, and it owns two profitable textile companies in Spain, two in Brazil, two in Mexico, and one each in India, Argentina, and Luxembourg. The Vatican is a heavy stockholder in these foreign companies, and in two instances holds the controlling shares. For 1966, when it showed a net profit of over $9.7 million, SNIA-Viscosa declared a dividend of 130 lire on each of its 46,703,125 shares. In 1967 when profits dipped substantially to only $310,000, the company nevertheless declared the same dividend of 130 lire but asked its stockholders to take into consideration the advisability of a merger with one of several possible companies that would provide diversification—now perhaps the most holy of words in Vatican business strategy.

One of the Vatican's biggest companies, Manifattura Ceramica Pozzi, which makes sinks, wash basins, toilet bowls, bidets, and other bathroom fixtures, has been in difficult straits during the last six years, reporting substantial losses each time. At the end of 1967, Pozzi came up with its smallest loss in recent years, $2 million. Adding that to the $11.9 million that Pozzi had dropped during the previous five years, the company's total deficits now have reached the sum of nearly $14 million. Thus it came as no surprise during 1968 when the Vatican sent in one of its ace troubleshooters, Count Enrico Galeazzi, to sit in on the board of directors as vice president.

With its capital listed at $36.96 million, Pozzi is nevertheless on a solid footing in Italy's economy. By diversifying into refractory materials, paints, plastics, and chemicals, the company—which is one of the oldest in Italy—is reorganizing its operation. During 1967 it completed the construction of a hygienic-sanitary fixtures plant for the Hungarian government and put into operation a new plant at Bizerte for Tunisia.

103

In addition to constructing the factories, the Pozzi firm trained personnel for them. Pozzi owns 90 percent of a company in France and 13⅓ percent of another company in Brazil, both of which have shown profits in the last two years. In Milan the Pozzi company holds 100 percent of the stock in the new Pozzi Ferrandina chemical plant, which went into operation in June 1967 with a capital of $18.1 million. With Count Galeazzi now bringing in his know-how, Pozzi officials expect to get back into the black again within a few years by escalating the $43 million export level of previous years.

One of the most ramified, fully Vatican-owned companies is Italgas, which has its main office in Turin. With a capital of almost $59.9 million, Italgas controls gas companies in thirty-six Italian cities, including Rome, Turin, Florence, and Venice. During the fiscal year 1967–8 it supplied 679 million cubic meters of home fuel to its customers and reported a profit of nearly $3.5 million.

Trending upward for over two decades, Italgas also controls a number of companies that are related to the gas industry. The Cledca Company (tar), Iclo (anhydrides), Funivie Savona San Giuseppe (iron ore and phosphorus), Fornicoke (coke for steel mills), Pontile San Raffaele (coke), Cokitalia (distillates), Società Acque Potabili di Torino (drinking water), Carbonifera Chiapello (real estate heating plants), Propaganda Gas (gas stoves), Urbegas (gas appliances), and La S.p.A. Forni ed Impianti Industriali Ingg. De Bartolomeis di Milano (industrial ovens). Of the last-named company, Italgas owns only 20.29 percent of the stock.

Not long ago I happened to mention to an American visitor that the Vatican owned a spaghetti factory in

Rome. My pun-loving friend immediately said, "The Vatican is getting rich making all that dough!"

Molini e Pastificio Pantanella, S.p.A., is a fully Vatican-owned company that packages various types of *pasta*. As a profitable sideline, Pantanella also produces *panettone* holiday cakes and an assortment of fifty-two different types of cookies. Backed by assets listed at $16.3 million, Pantanella reported a net profit of $290,562 for 1966 but broke even in 1967. The company would have done better, according to board director Marcantonio Pacelli, if it had not been for government-imposed regulations in July 1967, which not only placed cumbersome restrictions on the country's spaghetti factories but also controlled the price of soft and hard grains. But, as my friend might say, the Vatican is not at a loss for "grain" (Italian slang for money), for it owns outright, controls, or influences by its substantial though minority holdings all of the following companies which, according to the most recent financial statements, are in the black:

Società Mineraria del Trasimeno (mining—capital: $3.2 million), L'Istituto Farmacologico Serona (pharmaceuticals—capital: $1.4 million), La Società Dinamite (dynamite and ammunition—capital: $624,000), La Torcitura di Vittorio Veneto (yarn—capital: $800,000), Fisac-Fabbriche Italiane Seterie Affini Como (silk—capital: $3.4 million), Concerie Italiane Riunite di Torino (furs—capital: $4 million), Zuccherificio di Avezzano (sugar—capital: $1.6 million), Cartiere Burgo (paper products—capital: $23.2 million), Industria Libraria Tipografica Editrice di Torino (publishing—capital: $1.6 million), and Sansoni di Firenze (publishing—capital: $1.08 million).

The following companies, with which the Vatican has

a financial association of either major or minor degree, report a year-end loss or no profit as of this writing: Società Santa Barbara (mining—capital: $4.8 million), Caffaro Società per l'Industria ed Elettronica (chemistry and electronics—capital: $9.6 million), La Salifera Siciliana (salt—capital: $1.1 million), La Società Prodotti Chimici Superfosfati (chemicals—capital: $244,800), Bottonificio Fossanese (buttons—capital: $480,000), Saici Società Agricola Industriale per la Cellulosa Italiana (cellulose —capital: $24 million), Cotonificio Veneziano (cotton—capital: $3.2 million), Lanificio di Gavardo (wool—capital: $1.4 million), Fabbriche Formenti (textiles—capital: $104,000 [reduced from $1.04 million]), Sacit (ready-to-wear clothing—capital: $256,000), Molini Antonio Biondi di Firenze (spaghetti—capital: $960,000), C.I.T. (travel and tourism—capital: $800,000), and C.I.M. (department stores—capital: $1.2 million).

So much for private enterprise.

The question now arises, Does the Vatican have a stake in operations run by the state? The answer, not surprisingly, is in the affirmative. Let's look at another aspect, unique by American standards, of the Italian economy— that of the state as a rival and competitor of private entrepreneurs.

In the postwar period Italy's pell-mell economic expansion has had, at times, to walk a tightrope. Coming out of its catastrophic fascist cocoon, the Boot's economy went from rags to Vespas to Fiats—thanks in no small part to the heavy investments of the Vatican. Italy's gross national product pole-vaulted 143 percent in the period between 1953 and 1963 to $45.1 billion. Last year the G.N.P. reached over $66 billion at constant prices and was expected by the end of 1968 to boost itself another 5.5 percent to over $70 billion. To understand how Vatican money has benefited the Italian economy, one must understand the structure and function of Italy's Istituto di Ricostruzione Industriale. I.R.I., as it is affectionately known, is a public law corporation to which the Italian government assigns specific entrepreneurial functions. I.R.I. controls 130 firms, each of which is a share company that is run by the same rules as any private company in Italy.

What makes I.R.I. unique is that it has brought under government domination a vast complex of industries—and these include not only television and radio, railroads, airlines, and shipping, but also industries like steel, automobile manufacturing, and banking. I.R.I., which is therefore in competition with private industry, has over three hundred thousand people on its payroll. Its rate of investment is equivalent to nearly $3 million a day; its annual turnover, almost $3 billion; and the value of its industrial complex, about $12 billion.

Established in 1933, after the 1929 Wall Street crash set off a chain reaction in Europe, I.R.I. had two jobs: (1) to save the Italian banks, which had acquired shares in Italian industries that were in serious difficulty and, for that reason, were unable to guarantee the safety of their clients' deposits; (2) to put the finances of Italy's industry in order. It took almost five years to accomplish these tasks. But, in the end, credit was restored, and industry returned to life. The Italian government then took a second look at I.R.I. and, coming to realize that the giant, state-controlled industrial complex had been a daring financial experiment that had succeeded under the most difficult of conditions, decided to make it a permanent institution.

For every lira received from the state, I.R.I. companies have to raise another twelve from private investors. Since none of the I.R.I. companies could possibly finance its operations with its own capital, I.R.I. issues bonds on the open market. To date, nearly a half million Italian investors have put their money into I.R.I.'s issues. The biggest single investor has been the Vatican. There is no way of pinning down how much money the Vatican's financial advisers have tossed into I.R.I. operations, but the areas into which the Vatican has plunged most heavily are now known. Strictly for the record, let it be stated that in no case has the Vatican managed to become a majority shareholder in an I.R.I. company, despite the fact that in certain companies it is the largest single investor. It must be remembered, however, that since the Vatican's political party (the Christian Democrats) has been in control of the Italian government for over twenty years, the moving parts of the Italian state and its I.R.I. operation are well lubricated by Church money.

Critics of I.R.I. have accused it of being one of the main bottlenecks of Italy's economy. The criticism actually extends beyond I.R.I. to the Italian government and to the Vatican itself. Lack of business confidence during the middle sixties has held down private investment. In fact, in recent years, private companies have only been able to raise very small amounts through stock issues. Today I.R.I. and other government enterprises account for 40 percent of all Italian investments. Private enterprise is keenly aware of the competition. I.R.I. has long maintained, however—and the Vatican has backed it all the way—that it has never kept private industry from doing anything it has wanted to, either by absorbing all available capital or in any other way. But often, where private industry has been reluctant, I.R.I. has not.

I.R.I. has been carrying on a flirtation with U.S. business in recent years. Several of America's largest industrial concerns are tied in with I.R.I. subsidiaries. The U.S. Steel Corporation holds a 50 percent share in two I.R.I. steel plants. Armco International has a half interest in another. Raytheon and the Vitro Corporation have a stake in two of I.R.I.'s most calculated ventures in electronics. Siderexport, an I.R.I. trading subsidiary, has a 50 percent holding in Dalminter of New York.

The Vatican owes its current favorable position in I.R.I. to Bernardino Nogara, who foresaw a high return on the enormous investment he made in the state's industries. It is said that Nogara was considerably stimulated by the report of the governor of the Banca d'Italia at the end of the war. The report included the words, "We have reached a turning point. There is an arduous and fatiguing road that goes upward, and another, flat and easy, which leads to ruin."

Bewildered as Italy may have been by the extensive destruction of its factories and other industrial installations, Nogara's sights were clear. Italy would have to choose the first road and start on reconstruction immediately. What better place to invest the Vatican's money than the government's Finsider steel group? Although its plants were smouldering in ruins, Finsider gave promise of exceptional development once a rebuilding program was under way.

At the beginning of the postwar period, Finsider had an annual output of less than a million tons of steel. Today it produces ten million tons a year. By contributing decisively to making Italy self-sufficient as far as iron and steel requirements are concerned, Finsider has made an essential contribution to Italy's development, and has become one of the pillars of the nation's economy. With over 76,000 employees, and with an annual payroll of over $285 million, the company reports an annual profit of more than $24.1 million.

Finsider's objectives were given effective stimulus when the European Coal and Steel Community was set up. The Vatican and the Christian Democratic party both recognized the advantages to be gained by joining this organization. By putting an end to the protectionism that had characterized Italy's steel industry, the country entered into direct competition with the biggest steelmakers in the world, and is now the world's seventh largest steel producer.

Finsider's great strength today comes through its ownership of subsidiary companies. It owns, for instance, 51.6 percent of the Italsider Company, which produces pig iron, steel ingots, hot and cold rolled products, and welded pipes. Finsider is also a majority shareholder in the Dalmine Company, which specializes in steel ingots and seamless and welded pipes. Ninety-seven percent of the Terni Company stock is held by Finsider. Terni produces steel ingots, hot and cold rolled products, castings, forgings, and drop forgings. In addition, Finsider holds full or controlling interests in some twenty other connected or related companies.

The greatest amount of Vatican money in any I.R.I. company is probably in the Alfa Romeo automobile company (capital: $72 million). Italy's second largest producer of motorcars, Alfa Romeo makes about seventy-five thousand vehicles a year; by 1971, with the help of a new $500 million complex at Naples, it hopes to be producing more than a quarter of a million cars annually. Alfa Sud, the new plant in Italy's southland, had been a point of contention between Fiat, which controls about three fourths of the Italian car market, and I.R.I. It pitted Fiat president Gianni Agnelli squarely against I.R.I., the Italian government, the Christian Democratic party, and the Vatican, which are jointly trying to encourage the building of new industrial plants in Italy's depressed economic regions. Fiat termed the Alfa Sud factory "an economic error." Instead of putting up a new auto plant at Naples, Agnelli said, Alfa Romeo and its parents (I.R.I. and the Vatican) should join Fiat in other undertakings, such as building up an aircraft industry. The major growth phase of the European auto market was coming to an end, he argued, and there would be danger of overproduction in the nineteen-seventies. Agnelli lost his war.

Although the Vatican's biggest I.R.I. investment may be in Alfa Romeo, a considerable amount of papal money is also at work in Finmeccanica, the I.R.I. holding company that coordinates and finances I.R.I.'s engineering activities. There are thirty-five companies in Finmeccanica. In addition, Finmeccanica has a minority participation in thirty-two other companies, whose activities are ancillary; the Vatican holds the controlling interest in a few of these.

With all its affiliated companies, Finmeccanica is the biggest industrial concern in Italy, operating in almost every branch of the engineering industry—automotive and electrical engineering, electronics, design of aircraft and of railway cars, of heavy machine tools and of precision instruments, of heating equipment and of modern armaments (especially armored vehicles and tanks). Aided by heavy Vatican investments, the Finmeccanica group

111

has shown remarkable progress since 1959, when its annual profits began to rise from $185.6 million to the present-day figure of over $420 million (and its exports from $41.6 million a year to nearly $100 million).

Vatican money has also found its way into Finmare, another I.R.I. holding company, which is responsible for the country's most important passenger shipping lines (like the well-known Italian Line, and the Lloyd Triestino, Adriatica, and Tirrenia lines). With its ancient seafaring tradition and large tourist industry, Italy has never undervalued the importance of its ships. Accounting for almost 70 percent of the nation's passenger service, Finmare ships rank second in the number of passengers carried on the European–North American run and first on the South American route. With a capital of $28.8 million, Finmare, which has over ninety ships, totaling more than 700,000 tons, transports nearly two million passengers annually and carries more than 1.9 million tons of freight a year; the gross income is approximately $150 million per year. The Finmare-controlled Italian line has two ships, the 45,933-ton *Raffaello* and the 45,911-ton *Michelangelo,* crossing the Atlantic between North America and Europe, and it is certain that Vatican funds went into the total amount of money needed to finance the construction of these two luxurious liners.

The extent of the Vatican's investment in and control of Italy's main telephone company cannot be accurately ascertained, but it is safe to say that both are considerable and that Vatican influence has made S.T.E.T. (Società Finanziaria Telefonica) the respected and solid organization it is. At its last stockholders' meeting in July 1968, S.T.E.T. closed out its books with a declared net profit of $20 million for the second year in a row. Having recently increased its capital by $16 million, S.T.E.T. today is worth $304 million. With more than six million telephones, double the number in operation in 1958, S.T.E.T. today employs fifty-eight thousand persons. By 1970 it expects to have invested a total of $1.12 billion in new facilities and equipment and to have increased the number of its employees to sixty-eight thousand.

S.T.E.T. has also managed to spread itself into other companies. It is the sole or majority stockholder in many of these. In SIP-Società Italiana per l'Esercizio Telefonico (telecommunications), it holds 53 percent of the shares; in Società Italiana Telecommunicazioni Siemens, 98 percent of the shares; in Italcable (cables and telegrams), 60 percent of the shares; in SETA-Società Esercizi Telefonici Ausiliari, 99.99 percent of the shares; in FONIT-CETRA (phonograph records), 99.99 percent of the shares; in EMSA-Società Immobiliare per Azione, 52 percent of the shares; in SAIAT-Società Attività Immobiliari Ausiliarie Telefoniche, 100 percent of the shares; in CSELT-Centro Studi e Laboratori Telecommunicazioni, 100 percent of the shares; in SAGAS-Società per Azione Grandi Alberghi e Stazioni Climatiche, 100 percent of the shares; in SEAT-Società Elechin, Ufficiali degli Abbonati al Telefono, 100 percent of the shares. The S.T.E.T. group is also a minority stockholder in RAI-Radiotelevisione Italiana (22.9 percent), Telespazio (33.33 percent), Ates-Componenti Elettronici (20 percent), SIRTI-Società Italiana Reti Telefoniche Interurbane (10 percent), GE MI NA Geomineraria Nazionale (33.33 percent), SIEO-Società Imprese Elettriche d'Oltremare (11.09 percent), and SAGAT-Società Azionaria Gestione Aeroporto Torino (4.5 percent).

The Vatican is also involved in Italian banking. The country's three leading banks—Banca Commerciale Italiana, Credito Italiano, and the Banco di Roma—though belonging to the I.R.I. group, are closely tied to the Vatican. Together with a Vatican-owned bank, the Banco di Santo Spirito, they hold more than 20 percent of all bank deposits in Italy, have financed 50 percent of all foreign trade transactions, and placed two thirds of the new share and bond issues on the Italian stock exchange.

Two years ago, the Banca Commerciale Italiana, Credito Italiano, and the Banco di Roma decided to double their capital, by issuing shares against new money, so as to improve the ratio between their own resources and deposits. In the case of the Banca Commerciale Italiana, this raised the capital from $32 million to $64 million; in the case of Credito Italiano, from $24 million to $48 million; and in the case of the Banco di Roma, from $20 million to $40 million. In the last few years the time deposits and clients' current accounts of these three banks rose by hundreds of millions of dollars to a total that surpasses $6 billion (nearly 20 percent of the national total).

As for the Banco di Santo Spirito, which was founded by Pope Paul V in 1605, and which is one of the oldest banks in the world, its social capital is set at $12.8 million. From a 1966 total of $667 million, the bank hiked its total deposits last year to $729 million and reported a net profit for 1967 of $1.24 million, an increase of $226,000 over the previous year.

Although the four aforementioned banks have their main offices in Rome, the Vatican's real banking strength lies in the north of Italy. Cumulatively the Vatican's northern banks—particularly in the provinces of Lombardy, Veneto, and Emilia—are in even better health than the thriving four in the Eternal City. Foremost of these banks in the thigh part of the Boot is the Banco Ambrosiano in Milan, which was founded in 1896 and has a capital of $6.24 million. At the end of 1967 the Banco Ambrosiano reported a net profit of $1.4 million, which was virtually the same amount (give or take pennies) it had declared for the preceding period, and paid a dividend of 220 lire for a total of $1.056 million on three million shares, a repeat of the previous year.

The Banco Ambrosiano recently bought interests in three foreign fiscal organizations—the Banca del Gottardo di Lugano (Switzerland), the Kredietbank S.A. Luxembourgeoise (Luxembourg), and Interitalia (Luxembourg). Because the Italian parliament has not at this writing passed a bill to set up Italian investment funds (one such bill was introduced in 1964), the aforementioned Vatican-controlled fiscal societies have been providing a service whereby Italians can acquire shares of foreign mutual funds. At the end of 1967, foreign mutual funds from Italian investors through over-the-border holding companies totaled close to $4.5 million. Now two more Vatican-owned banking organizations—the La Centrale holding company and the Banca Provinciale Lombarda—have joined the lucrative business of purchasing shares from foreign investment trusts in the Swiss and Luxembourg markets. In addition, the Banca Provinciale Lombarda has recently joined with the Dutch Robeco and the German Concentra investment trusts to help Italians acquire shares of foreign mutual funds. Until a common investment-fund law is passed by the government, the foreign companies tied to the Vatican banks and investment companies will continue to operate profitably on the Italian market.

The Vatican's northern banking affairs have become so intricate today that it's almost impossible to explore their many ramifications. In an effort to provide some kind of clarity, we will not refer to those banks that have a capital of less than $80,000, and we'll divide the others into three categories. In the first are seven large banks that are owned outright by the Vatican: the Banco Ambrosiano of Milan, the Banca Provinciale Lombarda, Piccolo Credito Bergamasco, Credito Romagnolo, Banca Cattolica del Veneto, Banco di San Geminiano e San Prospero, and Banca San Paolo. In the second category are thirteen banks in which the Church holds a heavy interest but not necessarily a controlling one: the Banca Nazionale dell'Agricoltura, Banca di Credito e Risparmio di Roma, Banca Popolare di Bergamo, Banca Piemonte di Torino, Banca del Fucino di Roma, Banca Romana, Banca Torinese Balbis e Guglielmone, Banca dei Comuni Vesuviani, Istituto Bancario Romano, Banca di Trento e Bolzano, Credito Mobiliare Fiorentino, Banca del Sud, and Credito Commerciale di Cremona. In the third category are sixty-two banks in which, although the Vatican interest is minimal, that interest is protected by one or more Vatican agents on the board or at the policy-making level; among the bigger banks in this category are the Banca Popolare Cooperative di Novara, Credito Varesino, Credito di Venezia e del Rio de La Plata, the Banca Agricola Milanese, the Banca Toscana, the Banca Popolare di Milano, the Banca Emiliana, the Banco di Chiavari e della Riviera Ligure, Credito Bresciano, and the Banca Popolare di Verona.

Finally, it must be mentioned that thousands and thousands of small rural banks spread all over Italy are owned 100 percent either by the Vatican or by the local parish church, which submits to Vatican controls and regular audits by a peripatetic Vatican financier. Many of these small banks are located in the south and on Italy's two major Mediterranean islands, Sicily and Sardinia. As far as is known, the Vatican has control of only two large banks in this area—the Banco di Napoli and the Banco di Sicilia.

During 1967 eight banks bought by Italmobiliare, a financial institution owned by the Vatican's Italcementi cement company, merged to give life to a new Istituto Bancario Italiano (I.B.I.). Italmobiliare, claiming reserves of close to $9 million and showing a 1967–8 profit of $642,000, is headed by Carlo Pesenti—sometimes viewed as Italy's most knowledgeable banker, and certainly one of the Vatican's most trusted captains in the field. Serving also as Director General of Italcementi, Pesenti bought the banks for Italmobiliare one at a time over a five-year period. In what some consider one of the most brilliant financial maneuvers in Italy's *dopoguerra* economic history, Pesenti almost singlehandedly created the Istituto Bancario Italiano by having the Credito di Venezia e del Rio de La Plata (which he had acquired)—its capital is listed at $4.8 million—incorporate Pesenti's other seven banks—namely, Banca Torinese Balbis e Guglielmone (capital: $2.4 million), Banca di Credito e Risparmio di Roma (capital: $2.4 million), Istituto Bancario Romano (capital: $800,000), Banca di Credito Genovese (capital: $1.12 million), Banca Romana (capital: $2.4 million), Credito Mobiliare Fiorentino (capital: $1.12 million), and Banca Naef-Ferrazzi-Longhi of La Spezia (capital: $640,000). Ranking among the first twenty in the list of Italian banking institutions, thanks to cumulative deposits surpassing $512 million and a capital and reserve sum of $22 million, the new I.B.I. made quite an impact for an "infant" by reporting a profit of $800,000 during its first year of operation (1967).

Pesenti, who has control over two other important banking establishments (the Banca Provinciale Lombarda and the Credito Commerciale di Cremona) is serving as president of the newly founded bank, while Massimo Spada takes on the duties of vice president. The creation of I.B.I. will be only the first in a complex series of mergers of Vatican banks. The next merger will be that of the Banca Provinciale Lombarda and the Credito Commerciale di Cremona; it will result in the creation of a banking combine that will have over $1.28 billion in deposits—making it the largest private banking concern in Italy and one of the largest in all Europe, including Switzerland.

Vatican banking, however, is not confined to Italy. Funds managed by the Vatican's Prefecture of Economic Affairs are deposited in numerous non-Italian banks. Some are in America, and many are in Switzerland, where the Vatican maintains its funds in numbered accounts. Nobody really knows how much money the Vatican has in Swiss vaults. But it is known that one reason why the Vatican likes to bank in Switzerland is because the Swiss franc can provide protection against inflation and devaluation of money in other countries. Since 1945, there have been more than 170 currency devaluations all over the world—twelve of them in Brazil alone. Unlike the American dollar or the British pound, which have substantially less than 50 percent backing in gold reserves, the Swiss franc is guaranteed up to 130 percent by gold. So, because Switzerland's money is "hard money," the Vatican holds the francs and exchanges them for the legal tender of another country when needed.

The Vatican also uses its Swiss accounts to maintain its anonymity when gaining control of foreign corporations. Swiss banks, unlike American banks, can act as stockbrokers; they hold large numbers of shares belonging to clients but not in the clients' names. The Vatican, like any other depositor, can have a Swiss bank buy shares in a company in the bank's name and can thus obtain control of the company in full anonymity. The "Gnomes of Zurich"—a pet name pinned on Swiss banking officials by the British—point out, however, that the total number of shares their banks hold in U.S. companies is less than 1 percent of America's outstanding stock. Any speculation about how much the Vatican may have silently invested in the U.S. economy, at least at the corporation level, must take this figure into account.

Since Helvetian banking practices are based on secrecy, a style to which Vatican financiers are indeed no strangers, the Vatican and I.R.I., acting as major shareholders, operate the Banque de Rome Suisse, a Swiss offshoot of the Banco di Roma. This bank lists a $15.2 million capital stock; subject to Swiss laws, it keeps the names of its depositors clad in the impenetrable armor of legality.

A significant part of the Vatican's calculated diversification program is concerned with the rarely publicized activities of its various special credit institutes. The precise determination of the Vatican's stake in Italy's credit system would require an enormous amount of time and digging. But it can be calculated that of the some 180 medium- and long-term special credit institutions operating in Italy, at least a third are fed by Vatican money.

119

It should be noted that long-term loans constitute a highly important source of financing for expansion programs, and in this respect Vatican money has done much to shore up small and medium-sized businesses, which have the greatest difficulty in raising funds directly on the financial market, and has served the cause of a balanced growth of Italy's postwar economy. In this connection, mention should be made, albeit briefly, of two important aspects of this activity: (1) the significant financial support the Vatican's special credit institutes have been extending, particularly in recent years, to the process of industrialization in the depressed southland, and (2) the considerable assistance the Vatican's credit program is providing for the penetration of Italian industries into foreign markets.

The special credit institutes extend medium- and long-term credit. Each serves a particular sector of the economy, providing credit for industry, for example, or for public utilities companies or real estate companies or farmers or motion picture producers. Some of these institutes operate on a national scale, while others are limited to individual regions; some extend both medium- and long-term credit, while others specialize in medium-term transactions. Together with Italy's banks, the special credit institutes are the major source of new capital, and they provide most of the loans and the capital for the acquisition of securities.

One of the largest of these financial societies is La Centrale. Just what percentage the Vatican has of the equity of La Centrale is not known. It is known, however, that La Centrale is wedded to the Pirelli rubber company, which no doubt exercises direct controls over the agency. Just how much influence the Vatican has on its operations has not yet been made clear, though its control is widely accepted in the Italian business community.

The area in which La Centrale has been most prominently engaged is that of electric power, but since the time the Italian government nationalized the power companies, La Centrale has successfully sought to shift its strength into agriculture, mining, engineering, and trade organizations, both in Italy and abroad. Today its capital totals $107.3 million. La Centrale's assets are $276.8 million, of which $116.16 million are invested in the shares of some fifty-five companies and almost $60 million are out in loans to these companies. In addition, $156 million have been extended in credits to E.N.E.L., the national electric agency of Italy. La Centrale closed out 1967 showing a net profit of over $16.5 million.

During 1967, the Vatican-controlled Romana Finanziaria Sifir, S.p.A., fused with La Centrale and brought with it a stock capital of $72 million. Sifir's total assets were $168 million, of which $17.6 million were invested in the shares of thirty-six other companies and $22.4 million were out in loans to these organizations. Add to that the $70.4 million that have been extended in credits to E.N.E.L. and one gets a better picture of La Centrale's new associate.

One credit institution that is owned fully and outright by the Vatican is the Società Finanziaria Industriale e Commerciale, with a capital of $480,000. Other special credit institutes owned partially or controlled by the Vatican are La Società Capitolina Finanziaria (capital: $400,000), Credito Fondiario (capital: $16 million), Società Mineraria del Predil (capital: $384,000), Il Finanziario Investimento Piemonte (capital: $182,800), Società Finanziaria Italiana di Milano (capital: $400,-

000), Fiscambi di Roma e di Milano (capital: $1.6 million), Efibanca-L'Ente Finanziario Interbancario (capital: $16 million), and La Sind di Milano (capital: $1.6 million).

A number of insurance companies are Vatican owned; others are merely controlled by the apostolic financiers. Two important companies that fall into the former group are the Assicurazioni Generali di Trieste e Venezia (capital: $23.2 million), which turned a profit in 1967 of over $4.67 million, and the Riunione Adriatica di Sicurtà (capital: $6.9 million), which reported a profit of better than $1.27 million. Tied to the Banca Commerciale Italiana (which the Vatican controls), Assicurazioni Generali has a large portfolio of shares in Montecatini Edison, while Montecatini Edison has a large portfolio of shares in Assicurazioni Generali. Similarly, the Riunione Adriatica di Sicurtà, which is tied to the Credito Italiano bank (under Vatican control), has a working relationship with the La Centrale and Bastogi special investment institutes, both of which are under Vatican influence, and works closely with the Vatican's Italcementi cement company.

In violation of Italian laws, which prohibit members of the country's parliament from having business ties with any commercial enterprise, four senators (all Christian Democrats), one of whom was a minister several times, are on the board of directors of Assicurazioni Generali. Far from being unduly disturbed by this, the company and its associate Riunione Adriatica di Sicurtà have calmly conducted their affairs, and have done well. Over the years, they have profited from large insurance contracts involving government industries that deal in foreign trade, from indemnification against damage by nuclear bombardment and losses due to foreign nationalizations and confiscations of industries, and from various insurance programs written, with close state cooperation, for customers abroad. Over the years, Assicurazioni Generali and Riunione Adriatica, two companies that apparently do not see any ethical problems raised by having state officials represent their private interests, have become the two leading insurance companies in Italy.

Following is a list of other Italian insurance companies that are connected with and to the Vatican; in parentheses is each company's capital.

La Compagnia di Roma, also known as Riassicurazioni e Partecipazioni Assicurative (capital: $960,000); L'Unione Italiana di Riassicurazione (capital: $960,000); Assicurazioni d'Italia (capital: $2 million); Fiumeter (capital: $1.68 million); Compagnia Tirrena di Capitalizzazioni e Assicurazioni (capital: $2.4 million); L'Unione Finanziaria Italiana (capital: $640,000); Finanziaria Tirrena (capital: $160,000); Lloyd Internazionale (capital: $800,000); Fata-Fondo Assicurativo Tra Agricoltori (capital: $1.2 million).

The foregoing details provide an uncomfortably sharp realization that the Vatican and its men have indeed carved a niche for their firm in the world of big business.

This is no small accomplishment. After years of soul-searching, it has been decided, infallibly, that the accumulation of money is no more reprehensible, no more sinful, than the collecting of coins. True, the Vatican pays *ad perpetuum* lip service to poverty. But it doesn't practice it.

The Vatican apparently does not subscribe to the thesis that the enrichment of one man necessarily impoverishes

123

another. Indeed, taken in its proper perspective, the Vatican drive to make money has been highly beneficial to Italy. It has spurred Italy's material progress and helped the country recover from the battered state it found itself in after the war. It has produced capital for investment. It has generated wealth from which nearly everyone has gained. In a free society, which needs concentrations of private wealth to counterbalance the power of the state, the Vatican—which is no longer seeking territorial aggrandizement—has rendered a service to the theories of capitalism and provided impressive guidelines for those who believe in money and who worship at the altar of big business. The Apostolic Palace and Wall Street are singing a remarkably similar tune.

Because of the secrecy of the Church's complex business operations, the public image of the Vatican still remains ecclesiastical. The revelation of the Church as a big business often upsets people who should know better. Former Rome correspondent Barrett McGurn once reported the astonishment of U.S. Secretary of Labor James Mitchell after a visit with Pope Pius XII. McGurn interviewed Mitchell immediately after the visit. "The Pope knew all about the International Labor Organization," Mitchell said, surprised, "and he was already aware that the recession in the United States is over. Why, we've just learned that ourselves!"

How the Vatican
Takes Stock of
the Market
IX

IT ALL STARTED in 1962. . . .

The center-left coalition government under Premier Amintore Fanfani wanted at long last to end the preferential tax treatment Italy had been giving stockholders. In 1962, Fanfani established a dividend tax (called *cedolare*). Determined and sincere as he was, however, he tried to provide an exemption for the Vatican. It didn't work.

For the first part of 1963 the Vatican, like other shareholders, paid tax.

In April 1963 there were elections, and the Fanfani cabinet went down to defeat. It was replaced by Giovanni Leone's all-Christian Democrat "caretaker" cabinet. Leone's representatives began quiet talks with the Vatican, and shortly before its ouster in October, the Leone cabinet, in an exchange of diplomatic notes with the State of Vatican City, agreed that the new tax was not to be levied on dividends paid to the Vatican. Minister of Finance Mario Martinelli (Christian Democrat) forthwith sent a circular letter to the tax-collecting agencies, mostly banking institutions, informing them of the exemption that had secretly been granted to the Vatican on the basis of diplomatic negotiations between the two countries.

What followed was perhaps even more incredible. The new finance minister, Roberto Tremelloni (Social Democrat), read the diplomatic notes and the circular letter signed by his predecessor, and with the solid support of the new deputy prime minister, Pietro Nenni (Socialist), and the minister of the treasury, Antonio Giolitti (Socialist), refused to go along with the preferential arrangement. For months thereafter, Prime Minister Aldo Moro (Christian Democrat), sought a compromise; he asked the Vatican to submit a statement of its holdings as a prelude to obtaining an exemption. But Vatican Secretary of State Amleto Cardinal Cicognani refused, asserting that one sovereign government does not tell another about the state of its finances. Premier Moro retaliated by resorting to an old fighter's trick—holding back and waiting for the clock to run out. It worked—up to a point.

Interest in the Vatican's stock market practices was aroused by the Italian government's 1962 decision to levy a dividend tax (*cedolare*). This *cedolare,* which the paying office or the bank withholds on behalf of the government, is either 5 percent or 30 percent, depending on whether the stockholder records the securities with the tax office or chooses to remain unknown to the tax officials. The Vatican's disputed exemption from it brought about the events we outlined at the beginning of this chapter.

After the Moro government toppled in mid-1964, and was succeeded by yet another Moro government, the new minister of the treasury, Giovanni Pieraccini (Socialist), also declined to ratify the Vatican's exemption. In Italy, 1964 was a year when the business barometer was falling. The Vatican took advantage of this by threatening to dump several hundred million dollars' worth of shares on the Italian stock market. This, if the Vatican had done it, would have seriously depressed the market and inflicted irreparable wounds on Italy's already ailing economy.

Adding to Moro's worries during this period was the resignation of President of the Republic Antonio Segni, for reasons of ill health. A campaign had already begun to have a non-Christian Democrat named to fill the semi-honorary post. (Later, in fact, Giuseppe Saragat, leader of the Social Democrats, got the nod.) By all reasonable standards, this was not the time to risk a tug-of-war with the Vatican over tax matters.

Some kind of deal was obviously made, because the Moro cabinet approved a bill, which was later signed by Tremelloni and Saragat, that ratified the Vatican's exemption from the dividend tax. Although Socialist Minister Pieraccini refused to countersign the bill, it reached the competent legislative committee and was to go to the parliament for approval. As a bill, it never got there, though the subject did come up from time to time, either in the form of a query by a parliamentarian or a newspaper article.

For several years, the matter lay dormant. Then, early in 1967, it was revived. The Vatican had not been paying any dividend taxes since April 1963. Among other papers, the leftist Rome weekly *L'Espresso* wanted to know why. *L'Espresso,* which called the Vatican "the biggest tax evader in postwar Italy," said that one fifteenth of all the stocks on the exchange were Vatican owned. Other pejorative reports in Italy's left-wing press claimed that the Vatican's investments on the Italian exchange were worth between $160 million and $2.4 billion, and that thanks to its questionable immunity from the dividend tax, the Vatican was saving anywhere between $8 million and $120 million (based on a 5 percent tax on the estimated "declared" worths of between $160 million and $2.4 billion) or between $48 million and $720 million (based on a 30 percent tax on said "undeclared" estimated worths). It must be remembered, however, that because the Vatican often uses so-called front companies, some of which do indeed record their securities with the tax office, or make their identity known to tax officials, and because other Vatican-controlled companies do not record their securities with the tax office, both the 5 percent and the 30 percent tax rates are in operation. No one as yet has been able to compile a list showing which companies are the "5 percenters" and which are the "30 percenters," but whichever classification they fall into, they have not, so far, paid the tax that other companies (and the individual investors) are paying.

[In January 1968, the Italian government extended for another year the *cedolare* tax exemption enjoyed by the Vatican since 1963. The extension was granted, according to the announcement made by a government spokesman, to discuss a bill pending in the Italian parliament. The spokesman said that if the bill is not approved during 1968, the Vatican will have to pay all unpaid taxes since 1963 when the exemption was granted.]

On the basis of *L'Espresso*'s estimate, which maintains that the Vatican owns one fifteenth of all the stocks on the Italian exchanges, the total value of the Vatican's stocks would come to $733 million. Using the 5 percent tax figure, on the one hand, the tax saving comes to $36 million, whereas with the 30 percent tax figure, on the other hand, the tax saving comes to $219 million.

Estimates of that kind, and others in the left-wing press (however exaggerated they appear at first blush), prompted Italy's Finance Minister, Luigi Preti (a Socialist), to make in March 1967, an unusual public statement on the floor of the Italian Senate—unusual because up to then no government official had ever ventured any specific statistics or figures on the subject of Vatican taxes. Debunking the claim of one particular newspaper, which had asserted the Vatican had saved $64 million on its dividend inflow since the disputed bank circular of 1963, Preti said that the Vatican had earned $5.22 million in Italian stock dividends in 1965. On these earnings, he explained, the Vatican, if it had paid the 30 percent *cedolare* tax, would have turned in $1.6 million in taxes. Preti also said that the Vatican investment, according to indications, came to probably $104.4 million. From Minister Preti's figures—which he never documented—it appears that, over the six years since 1963, the Vatican therefore has not paid in a total of $9.6 million in taxes on its security holdings in Italy.

The Vatican's reaction to Preti's revelation was twofold. Its press spokesman, Monsignor Fausto Vallainc, declared, "I have been authorized to give a 'no comment' answer. But if you want my personal view— *which is just that!*—the motive for the refusal to comment is obvious. It would not be opportune to air the matter while it is being discussed by members of Parliament."

Unofficially, other sources in the Vatican said that the figures that had been cited in the anticlerical press were "clearly baseless." Estimates of the Vatican's tax savings were "absurd beyond being false," one spokesman main-

129

tained, adding that the actual amount was closer to $160,000. The same man cited the provisions of the Lateran Treaty in which Italy recognized the Vatican as a sovereign independent state and exempted this state from Italian taxation. The Vatican's unofficial newspaper, *L'Osservatore Romano,* eschewing its usual ecclesiastical verbiage, said that the amount of money involved was irrelevant, for the money was "holy money, entirely earmarked for charity."

In July 1968, the question of Vatican taxes flared up once again. The new Leone Cabinet, though formed as a "baby-sitter" kind of government [See Chapter X], astonished everyone shortly before it won the confidence vote of parliament by a squeak. Premier Giovanni Leone, apparently in a gesture of appeasement to the left, a state-of-the-nation message that the Vatican would have to pay its tax arrears. Leone said that rather than granting a new tax exemption—which was due to expire toward the end of 1968—the government intended to let the exemption drop and not seek parliamentary ratification for a new bloc of exemptions.

Bluntly coming to their defense, Church officials issued a protest through the Holy See press office, implying that the Vatican felt strongly about retaining its tax-exempt status. Monsignor Vallainc, in his capacity as the spokesman, noted that the Vatican contributes heavily to Italy's income with its investments and tourist attractions. Moreover, he said, several other countries, including the United States, are giving the Roman Catholic Church tax exemptions because of its special nature and work. He reaffirmed the view that taxing the income of the Holy See, besides violating the acts that regulate church-state relations in

130

Italy, would take away money destined for religious and social work projects carried out by priests in Italy and in other parts of the world. The official statement Vallainc read contained this paragraph:

The counterpart of this tax exemption can be seen in the framework of reciprocity, in the wide contribution that the apostolic activity of the Holy See has on tourism, as well as in the advantages Italy derives from the Holy See's stock investments which contribute to increasing the national income.

Following still another Vatican blast against Premier Leone on the tax issue, Socialist Luigi Preti came back into the squabble by publicly rejecting the reasons listed by the Vatican to continue its tax-free privileges. He said:

It is true that Holy See activities are advantageous for the tourism influx to Italy and that this increases state incomes, but I cannot see why these should serve as reasons for the Vatican to be exempted from taxes. Also I think the Vatican has no grounds in pointing to the treatment it enjoys in other countries where the Holy See is exempt from taxes. The Italian law clearly indicates there are no exemptions for any foreigners having Italian stock holdings. The noble aims that the Holy See pursues here and elsewhere in the world are highly respected in Italy, and by all political parties, but this is no reason for tax-free treatment.

Curiously enough, the 1967 tax squabble did not bring to light the long history of Vatican "tax evasion." The record between 1929 (when the Lateran Treaty was signed) and 1962 is an interesting one. Let us examine this record, which up to now has been given no public attention.

Without entering into a long analysis, it is sufficient to repeat that the Concordat, the third document of the Lateran Treaty, provided for tax exemptions for "ecclesiastical corporations." During the nineteen-thirties and the early nineteen-forties, the Mussolini regime gave

131

added assistance to the Vatican treasury by way of special "dispensations." In October 1936, for instance, Mussolini imposed a 5 percent corporation tax to help underwrite a large loan needed to pay for the war in Abyssinia, and levied in addition, to absorb the interest costs on the war loan, a 3.5 percent tax on every thousand lire's worth of real estate holdings to run for a twenty-five-year period; Decree 1743 of October 5, 1936, set up this tax schedule, but Article 3 of the decree exempted the Vatican and Vatican companies from paying either of the two levies.

Vatican-owned companies were also exempted from a special duty ordered in October 1937. This required corporations to pay a graduated tax on their capital stock. The tax was originally levied on all corporations, but early in 1938, when the collection program got under way, a special order exempted those owned by the Vatican.

In 1940, Italy instituted a sales tax (I.G.E.). But, in a circular letter dated June 30, 1940, the finance minister freed the Vatican and all churches from paying it. The I.G.E. tax remains in existence to this day. So does the Vatican's exemption.

Lastly, in October 1942, a law was passed, "in the spirit of our Concordat," which exempted the Vatican from paying certain then-existing assessments on dividends. To make matters clearer, the finance minister, in a decree dated December 31, 1942, published an official roster that listed every organization that was not eligible for taxation on dividends. Nearly all of the organizations listed were Vatican affiliated.

The roster went unnoticed by the public because of the year-end holidays. It went unnoticed by the press because it was published not in the government's *Gazzetta Ufficiale* (*Official Gazette*), but in an obscure state bulletin called *Rivista di Legislazione Fiscale,* on page 1,963 of the second volume for 1943, a volume that appeared a considerable time after the beginning of the year.

Attempts to avoid taxes are nothing new in the history of Italy's stock exchange. The *borsa valori* has roots that go back to the Republic of Venice, where the first official exchange was set up in 1600. In early Italy, the *borsa* was often a square or street where all types of trading—in goods and services, in securities, in precious metals and money—were carried on. In the first half of the eighteenth century, the commodities markets were put on a formal basis; then, in the nineteenth century, separate exchanges were set up to handle securities. On February 6, 1808, Eugène de Beauharnais, viceroy of Italy and Napoleon's stepson, established the first official exchange in Italy, at Milan. Nine other Italian cities— Venice, Trieste, Turin, Rome, Palermo, Naples, Genoa, Florence, and Bologna—now have exchanges; but the one in Milan is still the largest.

By the turn of the century, Italy's first electric power companies had been formed, as had other public service companies, textile and chemical companies, and some companies devoted to heavy industry. Trading increased and more securities were listed. In 1901, the number of securities traded on the Milan exchange had risen to 102; 54 of these were common stocks. By 1938, 267 securities were traded at Milan; by 1960, 428. In the postwar years, the Milan and other Italian exchanges began to register appreciable volume; today, despite being small by American standards, the volume at the exchanges is heavy compared to what it was in the immediate postwar years. But public participation in trading is comparatively slight.

Few securities are owned by the Italian public. Many

are owned by the Vatican itself; and many others by banks and other financial institutions, by insurance companies and pension funds, and by industrial concerns—a number of which are controlled or owned by the Vatican.

Italy's small investors show a decided disinclination to buy common stocks. They prefer fixed-interest-bearing securities, especially those guaranteed by the government. Banks are called upon for heavy support of the securities market. In the last year for which a report is available, banks and institutional investors absorbed 48 percent of the new issues of common stocks and preferred stocks—and although the facts are unclear or fragmentary, a goodly part of this seems to have been done with Vatican capital. The quoted value of all Milan's securities, which represent more than three quarters of the total shares on all Italy's ten exchanges, generally stands at about $8.5 billion. In any given year, there is usually a turnover of a little less than 7 percent of the total shares; slightly under 260 million shares are traded, at a market value of slightly under $1 billion.

Another 1962 decision by the Italian government—that to nationalize the electric current industry—also aroused interest in Vatican finances. When the national electric agency, called E.N.E.L., was formed, it was learned that the special credit institute La Centrale, a Vatican-associated agency that specializes in electric power companies, had a portfolio of 8,235 shares (worth $24,801,600) in the Selt Valdarno electric works and 8,417 shares (worth $25,153,600) in the Romana di Elettricità Company; that another Vatican special credit institution, Bastogi, had 10,265 shares (worth $13,838,-400) in the Società Meccanica Elettrica electric company,

6,407 shares (worth $8,441,600) in the Finanziaria Adriatica company, 5,385 shares (worth $12,146,000) in the S.G.E.S. company, 4,013 shares (worth $10,038,-400) in Edison, 1,137 shares (worth $4,782,400) in the Elettricità Sarda, and 996 shares (worth $2,659,200) in Selt Valdarno. Payments on these holdings, by way of indemnity installments, are still being made by E.N.E.L. to La Centrale and Bastogi.

As one of the world's largest shareholders, the Vatican holds securities frequently quoted as being worth $5.6 billion. The sum is probably an understatement, for the Vatican has invested in exchanges throughout the world, and even a conservative estimate of its portfolio tends to show that the figure is in excess of $5.6 billion. According to an appraisal made by London's *Economist* a few years ago, the Vatican's Italian portfolio contains (as *L'Espresso* had earlier claimed) approximately one fifteenth of the total number of shares quoted on the ten Italian stock exchanges; the value of these shares, said *The Economist,* was $8.8 billion at the end of 1964. This would put the amount of capital invested by the Vatican in Italian stocks at around $586.6 million. But taking into consideration the current $11 billion value of Italy's ten exchanges and the fact that many of the stocks owned by the Vatican are held through front companies—banks, special credit institutes, and insurance companies—a more realistic estimate of Vatican penetration into Italy's stock market would place it between 40 and 50 percent of the total number of shares quoted on all of the Italian stock exchanges. Hence, this would bring the Vatican figure within the $5 billion range.

Improbable as this may seem at first glance, the fiscal truth has been kept hidden by the Vatican itself, by a sympathetic Italian press, and by the corps of foreign reporters in Rome. Deferring to the notoriously thin-skinned Vatican, most correspondents avoid the subject in their dispatches.

How long will the Vatican's "tax evasion" go on? The answer depends on the Vatican. Why? Because the pope is the dealer in this strange game of poker between the Vatican and the Italian state. But I think the pope may have overplayed his hand by attempting to bluff the Italian people—and may, before the next round, have to put his cards, and his blue chips, on the table.

The Vatican
in Politics
X

IN ITALY, the outstretched palm of the bribe-taker has become almost as familiar as the dinnertime plate of spaghetti. The venerable *bustarella*—literally, little envelope—slipped to government workers in exchange for favors has created ethical havoc between business and government.

The Italian version of payola flourishes in the thickets of cluttered bureaucracy, and the practice of *bustarella* often smacks of comic opera. It is perhaps not so amusing in the pharmaceutical field, where, by virtue of a curious Italian law, foreign drug companies are required to register the formula of any product they wish to market. The same law states that if a similar commodity is already being sold, then the foreigner cannot sell his product in Italy. The results are inevitable. No sooner does an American company register a formula than one of the Italian pharmaceutical houses pays somebody in the right office for the privilege of a peek at it. In no time at all, a duplicate product is on the shelves, usually under another name.

Many Italians believe that if you want to get something done, you play the game of *bustarella* in government offices—or you take money to the Vatican. The more cynical Italians will tell you that service is rendered in direct proportion to the thickness of the envelope. The hard truth about Italy's political system, particularly since the end of the war, is that the Catholic clergy, having direct access to the ministers and other key government figures, can usually get what it wants. An Italian who wants something done will usually go either to his parish priest or to the bishop of his diocese, who will, as often as not, intervene with a key cardinal—who has the right connections.

This brings to mind a friend of mine, a tenor, who approached, through the usual channels, a highly placed cardinal in the Vatican. The singer, thinking he would enhance his career immeasurably if he could have the honor of opening the season at one of Italy's major opera houses, asked the cardinal to get him the lead part for the first night. The cardinal suggested that a sum of approximately $32,000 might be appropriate—"for services rendered." My friend declined making the payment. Later, an American tenor snapped up the part. The American, traveling the same path as his Italian contemporary, had found the same prelate, whose interest in C-notes was more financial than musical.

In another case, the husband of a family friend was killed by an Italian army truck while he was sitting in his parked automobile. The widow easily won her suit against the Italian government, but payments on the $25,000 judgment never reached her. After fourteen years, and no payments, she enlisted the aid of a powerful cleric inside the Leonine Walls. His fee for "making the necessary phone call" came to approximately $12,000. Within six months the widow got all her money from the Italian state.

Informed Italians know where to go when they want to get something done. It's merely a matter of finding the right cog in the Vatican mechanism. The Italian people are well aware of how intertwined their government is with the Vatican, and the Vatican with their government. This is so because of the nature of Italian politics.

There was a time when the Vatican would have nothing to do with the ballot box. It is not difficult to discern that that time is now past. The Vatican, which has so far been content to manipulate indirectly rather than directly, plays politics in Italy partly because it wants to keep the Communist party at bay and partly because a heavy hand in the Italian cabinet and the twenty-six ministries is a kind of guarantee that the financial interests of the Church will be served.

Toward the end of World War II, the Vatican found it worthwhile to revive a conservative political party that had been founded by a priest, Don Luigi Sturzo, in 1919. The party, which was originally known as the Popular party, was reorganized with Vatican funds and skill and became the present-day Christian Democratic party, which has ruled Italy without interruption since the end of 1945.

The Vatican does not directly control the Christian Democrats, who are popularly known among the Italian people as *democristiani,* and also as *i preti*—literally, the priests. It does not give instructions to its men—but it doesn't have to. It does not express opinions on given political issues—but the party leadership is always aware of the Vatican's views. Ostensibly, Italy's is a secular government, but the rules of conduct are formulated by the

139

Vatican. For this reason, the Vatican has allowed only trusted practicing Catholics who will do the Church's bidding to rise to the top political jobs in Italy.

One might ask whether the success of the Vatican in Italian politics can be attributed to the merging of its secular and spiritual qualities. The answer is indeed in the affirmative. The Vatican alternately poses as a church and as a political force, depending upon which pose will prove more advantageous at the moment. At the lower levels, through the local congregations, the Church presents itself as a religious organization and wins support by religious appeals to its followers; often these appeals influence voters. At the higher levels the Church becomes increasingly a political organization and, indirectly, exerts a controlling influence over the affairs of the Italian state. The Church's chief instrument has been the *democristiani*, an army of faithful Christian Democratic politicians that has obviated the Vatican's need for maintaining powerful lobbies. Italy's postwar political history is intimately tied to *i preti*, under whom Italy has been carefully guided to its present position in the world of nations.

Italy is no doubt the better for it. But all has not been politically tranquil for the Vatican. After World War II, the Italian Communist party—a prime enemy of the Vatican—became the largest Red party outside the Iron Curtain, but now it appears to have been boxed in by Vatican forces.

Rebuilding a democratic political structure during the postwar era presented considerable difficulties for Italy, whose people had been denied any participation in the affairs of the country for over twenty years. The consequences were deeply felt between 1945 and 1947. Urgent measures were required to help Italy's economy, and it was apparent that decisive steps would have to be taken in the political field. It was during this period that the Vatican elected to go into politics on a full scale, though deliberately eschewing direct participation. The decision was doubtless prompted by the extreme left-wing parties that were seeking to impose their will on Italy through public demonstrations.

In a period when internal law and order was threatened by strikes and demonstrations, there arose the name of Alcide De Gasperi. De Gasperi, a former Vatican librarian and a devout Catholic, needed little encouragement from the Vatican to enter the political arena and steal the spotlight away from the revolutionary parties. In its own way, the Vatican took on the task of settling Italy's political unrest by pushing to the fore a man like De Gasperi, who would not only give help to a country badly in need of assistance but would also bring to it the social and economic equilibrium desired by the pope.

With courage and admirable political acumen, De Gasperi devoted himself to the material strengthening of his country. Although the shadow of the Vatican was always behind him, he could not and did not ostensibly cater to the immediate interests of his silent sponsors. Upon his appointment as prime minister in December 1945, he emerged as the strong man of Italian politics. By quieting the various factions that had blocked Italy's postwar democracy, he was able to call the first free elections the country had had in nearly a quarter of a century. The elections, held in June 1946, had the twofold objective of letting the people decide whether they wanted a monarchy or a republic, and of electing deputies to a constitutional assembly. The referendum showed twelve million votes in favor of a republic and ten million in favor of a monarchy. Umberto II, who had become king after the formal abdication of Victor Emmanuel III in May 1946, and who had reigned for only thirty-four days, removed himself from Italy under protest, to continue to campaign from abroad for the restoration of his throne. His downfall eliminated one of the last brakes on the power of the Vatican. Now the duties of the chief of state were placed in the hands of Prime Minister De Gasperi.

The elections, which brought on the collapse of a number of small parties, allowed the Christian Democratic party to emerge in full strength. When Italy's new parliament elected Enrico de Nicola the country's first interim president, Prime Minister De Gasperi forthwith resigned. De Nicola then asked him, as leader of the majority party, to form a new cabinet. Of the many important moves made by the second De Gasperi government, one that particularly deserves mention was the drawing up of a preliminary plan for agrarian reform. This had been one of the Christian Democratic party's—and the Vatican's —chief aims at the time. Many aspects of De Gasperi's agrarian plans have since been carried out.

A subsequent government crisis in 1947 led to the third De Gasperi government, known as the Tri-partite Government, because the cabinet consisted of *democristiani*, Communists, and Socialists.

In 1948, when Italy's new constitution came into force, elections were held for the first parliament. In the elections the Italian Communist party, which boasted an unprecedented membership of one and a half million, and which had formed a common electoral slate with the Socialists, made a concerted bid to take over the country.

Italy's survival of this take-over attempt marks one of the crucial points of its history.

Much of the credit for barricading the Reds in 1948 should go to the Vatican. The Church let out all the stops for that election—even to the extent of swinging open the doors of convents and marching cloistered nuns off to the polling places to vote for Christian Democrat candidates. In many instances where a *democristiano* won by only a few votes, it was the ballots cast by sisters who had been shepherded from their nunneries to an election booth that made the difference. With 92 percent of the country's eligible voters casting ballots, and with over a hundred parties presenting candidates, the elections gave the Christian Democrats an absolute majority of 306 seats in the Chamber of Deputies, a high-water mark in *democristiani* fortunes. The party also showed up strongly in the Senate, winning 131 seats. Had it not been for the 107 special "life senators" appointed under a special provision in the new constitution, this would also have constituted a true majority. In joint session both chambers met and elected Luigi Einaudi president of the republic. Once again, De Gasperi was asked to form a government.

In order to escape the stigma of Vaticanism, De Gasperi assigned some cabinet posts to the Liberals, Republicans, and Social Democrats. A four-party (Christian Democratic, Liberal, Republican, and Social Democratic) center coalition was thus formed. Under it, a politically stable five-year period ensued, during which the astute De Gasperi set about reconstructing and strengthening his regime. During this period monetary stability was attained, a start was made on new construction, new plans for agrarian reforms were introduced, and projects were launched to assist Italy's underdeveloped areas.

In May 1951, the first local elections were held. The results showed the sinew of the Christian Democratic party. A second national election took place two years later, in June 1953, and once more the *democristiani* won the majority of votes.

After heading a total of eight governments, De Gasperi finally fell, in August 1953, when a disagreement among the four parties made it impossible for him to obtain a majority for the new cabinet. In eight successive coalitions he had shown himself to be a great statesman who saw Italian politics polarized by the sharp conflict between red and black—the red banner of the Communists and the black cassocks of the priesthood.

The task now fell to another *democristiano*, Giuseppe Pella, whose government was essentially of a "caretaker" nature. But, with the development of the crisis over Trieste, Pella resigned. Mario Scelba (Christian Democrat) succeeded in re-establishing the alliance of the Christian Democratic, Liberal, Republican, and Social Democratic parties. The four-party government embarked on some farsighted political and administrative projects, negotiating the agreement that returned northern Trieste to Italy and passing new laws approving agricultural reforms, a modernized building code, and new public works. Keenly interested in the public works, the Vatican stood ready to offer the professional services of its construction companies to the government and to private builders alike.

When President Einaudi's term of office expired in April 1955, the parliament elected Giovanni Gronchi (Christian Democrat) to the office. Shortly thereafter, there followed still another government crisis, when a group of deputies broke away from the National Monarchist party and formed another monarchist party, and Premier Scelba resigned in June 1955. In July, Antonio Segni (Christian Democrat) formed a new cabinet, which was composed of the same four parties as the previous one. This coalition succeeded in bringing into being a new tax law—favorable to the Vatican—and a new ministry, the Ministry for State Participations, which was made responsible for controlling the operations of government-owned holding companies. The Segni government, with pontifical blessings, also initiated several important public works projects in the lower part of Italy and in the northern Po delta region.

In May 1957, a new cabinet was formed under Adone Zoli (Christian Democrat). Parliament eagerly approved the treaty of the European Economic Community, which made Italy one of the founding members of the Common Market. Important decisions were also made for Italy's depressed rural areas, and pensions for farm workers were approved. Premier Zoli stayed in power until shortly after the May 1958 elections, and, although *i preti* lost some ground and a number of seats in both houses, Amintore Fanfani (Christian Democrat) was charged with forming a new cabinet in July of that year. With center-left tendencies, the Fanfani cabinet, which included some members of the Social Democratic party, drafted a ten-year plan for the modernization and reconstruction of Italy's road network (the contracts went mostly to Vatican-owned companies), voted $64.5 million for a ten-year agricultural plan, elaborated a decade-long educational program, and adopted protective measures against abuses in the wholesale business.

Fanfani's efforts were continued by another cabinet, headed by Antonio Segni, who had previously been the premier from July 1955 to May 1957. Executing policies that encouraged industry and agriculture, Premier Segni brought on monetary stability and a balanced budget, reduced unemployment, and put into operation a vast public works program. But the political situation in Italy was changing and eventually led to a forty-day parliamentary crisis, after which Segni resigned. There followed the usual consultations with President Gronchi, and finally Fernando Tambroni (Christian Democrat) was given the task of forming a new government, consisting of Christian Democrats.

In July 1960, the Tambroni cabinet was replaced by one headed (again) by Fanfani. Fanfani managed to provide loans and other assistance for artisans and small industries, to modernize the telephone network, to reconstruct and bring up to date the national highway system, and to put into effect a five-year plan for agricultural development. He also was instrumental in pushing for more funds for the Southland Development Fund, which had been established to speed industrialization in the depressed regions.

Still another crisis brought the downfall of Fanfani's cabinet in 1962; nonetheless, Fanfani was called on to try his hand once again. He formed a cabinet with the famous *apertura a sinistra* (opening to the left). The cabinet, which included Social Democrats, fully adhered to the principles adopted by the Christian Democratic party at its congress in Naples the month before.

Nothing in Italian politics in the postwar era brought on such fiery discussions as did the so-called opening to the left—a policy that was adopted not because of any special philosophical theory, but because it gained the Christian Democrats the support of the non-Communist

146

left. Specifically, this meant the Christian Democrats would get cooperation not only from the Social Democrats but also from Pietro Nenni and his Socialist party. The Socialists—or, as they were more frequently referred to, the Nenni Socialists—had thirty-five seats in the Senate and eighty-four seats in the Chamber of Deputies. Although the new Fanfani cabinet did not include the Nenni Socialists, it had the assurance of Nenni that they would not vote against the Christian Democrats whenever the Prime Minister sought a parliamentary vote of confidence. During this Fanfani government, Foreign Minister Antonio Segni was elected president of the republic, replacing Gronchi, whose term had expired.

The Vatican's role during this period merits review. If the Vatican had not wanted its Christian Democratic party to work with the left-wing, Marxist politicians, then there would never have been an "opening to the left" in Italian politics; as members of a Catholic party, the *democristiani* were obliged to maintain their Vatican-approved principles, but the first law of all successful politicians is to retain a position of power. The *apertura a sinistra* became possible, thanks to a change of climate within the Vatican itself. Much of the change was attributable to Pope John XXIII, whose policies were in strong contrast to the stiffly anti-Communist ones of his predecessor, Pius XII.

Pope John, who made some public pronouncements that did not condemn the Communists outright, felt that the Vatican should stay out of Italian politics as much as possible. By keeping his hands off Fanfani's attempts to bring on the "opening to the left," he did the Vatican a service, for because of the "opening," the *democristiani* were able to remain in power. As one prominent journalist later said, "Pope John, by being a nonpolitical pontiff during this period, was indeed the most political of pontiffs, and it saved his Catholic party from who knows what!"

The *apertura a sinistra* worked well, although it was never without sharp criticism both from ranking *democristiani* and from the public at large. About this time Italy was undergoing a *miracolo economico,* and this boom helped the Fanfani cabinet consolidate its position. Among other things, it obtained the passage of some important school bills (which implemented a provision for eight years of compulsory education, provided free textbooks for elementary school children, and allocated $320 million to modernize and better equip schools and universities), increased social security payments, set standards to regulate the purity of food products, modernized the country's judicial system (which had hardly changed in a century), made large-scale expenditures to shore up Sardinia's economy, appropriated large sums to be spent over a ten-year period for the construction of hospitals, imposed a withholding tax on stock dividends (the Vatican was later—by the maneuver described in Chapter IX—exempted from paying this tax), imposed a new real estate tax that put a stop to land speculation in expanding suburban areas, provided financial assistance to needy university students, and nationalized the electric power companies. This last measure, a key item for the Nenni Socialists, was part of the price the *democristiani* had to pay for the Socialists' parliamentary backing.

Premier Fanfani and his cabinet went down to defeat in the 1963 national elections, in which the Catholic party lost a substantial number of seats. The man who

148

eventually succeeded Fanfani was Giovanni Leone, another Christian Democrat. Having formed a minority cabinet composed exclusively of *democristiani,* Leone ran a "caretaker" government until the political situation clarified.

In time, Aldo Moro, secretary of the Christian Democrats, took over and continued as prime minister until the May 1968, elections, having formed three straight center-left cabinets following one knockdown after another. In that election, though the Communist party made some gains (winning thirteen new seats at the expense of the United Socialist party—which had helped the Christian Democrats govern Italy for five years in the center-left coalition), the Christian Democratic party gained six new seats in the Chamber of Deputies (raising its total to 266) and two new seats in the Senate (bringing the total to 135).

In June, Senator Giovanni Leone, the middle-of-the-road Christian Democrat who had headed a stopgap government five years before, formed a minority cabinet composed of Christian Democrats in a political play with practically the same cast. This move was made when the Socialists refused to join in another center-left coalition because they blamed their May election loss of some two million votes on their having cooperated with the Christian Democrats. Until the Socialists had decided, at a party congress in November, whether to stay at the window or to rejoin the Christian Democrats in a renewed center-left partnership, the caretaker Leone government had to depend on uncertain support from other parties, or abstentions, to get any legislation enacted over the summer.

It appears that, although Italian governments have been

falling at a fairly brisk rate since the Vatican entered the political arena, the same eighty men have been playing "ministerial chairs." Nearly all of these eighty perennials are members of the Christian Democratic party. When Moro formed his third cabinet, only two of his twenty-six ministers were new; fifteen of the remaining twenty-four had served in the previous cabinet. Equally startling is the fact that, since July 25, 1943, when Benito Mussolini was arrested, Italy has had twenty-seven governments with a total of 588 ministerial posts, all of which have been held by only 181 men. Seventy men served only once, and thirty-two twice; thus the remaining 454 posts were shared by only seventy-nine men. This count gives only a partial picture of the durability of these politicians, for the numbers deal only with ministerial appointments and do not include the posts held by these same men as undersecretaries.

To understand, in part, how the Christian Democrats have managed to retain control for a quarter of a century, one must examine the role of Catholic Action in Italy. Conceived and organized by Pius XI soon after his ascension to the papacy in 1922, Catholic Action is a strong lay organization with a membership that numbers many hundreds of thousands. Although the organization's stated purpose is to promote Christian education and charitable enterprises, its various diocesan branches are also active in politics and cooperate in furthering the political doctrines of the Church. Catholic Action derives its strength from the fact that it is able to influence bureaucratic appointments, to place its men on the boards of directors of state-run industries, and to get its own people major academic chairs.

A good example of the role that Catholic Action plays

150

in Italy's political picture is provided by Catholic Action's activities in 1948. Almost certainly, Italy would have gone Communist in that year's election if organized Catholic Action groups had not been able to meet the Communists in a rough-and-tumble, head-on collision. Since the Christian Democratic party did not at that time have an inner structure that would have enabled it to ward off the extreme left, the Vatican called on the Catholic Action groups in the country's three hundred dioceses. The intervention of this network prevented the left from emerging from the election as the most powerful political force in Italy.

Whatever principles guide Catholic Action in Italy, it will not be hobbled by genteel considerations of democratic propriety. Politics in Italy, as everywhere else, is a dirty game—and Catholic Action will go to any lengths in order to exercise its power for the Vatican.

An official of the Socialist party's executive committee holds to the view that no other group in Italy is as powerful as Catholic Action. According to him, "Most of the major policies that have evolved in this postwar period have been policies favored by the Catholic hierarchy, or at least, policies that did not run strongly counter to the values of Catholicism." He continues:

> We all know that with Vatican approval the Catholic Action effort to create civic committees was responsible for the amazing victory registered by the Christian Democrats in the 1948 election. I am of the personal opinion that we would have in Europe today a different Europe—an entirely different Europe—had the Communists succeeded in winning that election. People in the Free World, particularly those in the United States, do not truly know just how crucial Italy's 1948 election was for the entire world. It transcended the borders of Italy. Indeed Catholic Action made the difference. Because the Vatican has these Catholic Action committees ready, the

151

Pope's power as a politician is tremendous. The committees can defeat Christian Democrats who do not cooperate, or at the very least, they can make the re-election of these individuals extremely difficult.

To understand Catholic Action's enormous power, it is necessary to recognize the extraordinary control Catholic Action has over Italy's women voters. Of the twelve million ballots guaranteed to the Christian Democratic party in a given election, seven million come from female voters, who are dominated by local Catholic Action workers.

Generally speaking, women in Italy have very little grasp of politics. But Italian women do have the right to vote. And local Catholic Action workers do not fail to take advantage of the situation.

One British author perhaps put his finger on it when he interviewed a Sicilian peasant and recorded her statement:

The cross bears us to heaven. Who does Padre Pietro tell us to vote for? Always for the cross [the symbol of the Christian Democratic party is a red cross emblazoned on a white elongated shield], for God knows how to reward us. My mother, paralyzed as she is—they carry her to vote—and I go into the room where you vote, and I put the sign for her, on the shield with the cross. I am not two-faced with God, I do not betray Him. Certainly, all of us make mistakes, and even in this party there are men who make them, but God looks after them. High-ups promise us a lot of things, make us hope, deceive us, and then give us nothing—but that isn't to say that one shouldn't vote for God. There are many priests in the Christian Democratic party, and there's the Pope himself, too—and how can these make mistakes?

The Vatican's Expenses

XI

IN THE SUMMER of 1962, Vatican officials received a letter from Mrs. Elina Castellucci, a seventy-nine-year-old woman who lived twenty miles outside of Florence. Contending to be a direct descendant of Michelangelo, the woman wrote that she had a "small" claim on the Sistine Chapel but that she was not asking for it to be paid. All she wanted was a check for 300 lire (48 cents) to pay for a ticket to the Vatican Museum so that she could see her great-great-great-great-great-great-grand-uncle's masterpiece.

"I would like the satisfaction of visiting the Sistine Chapel free," she told a reporter. "Why should I buy a ticket to see something a member of my family painted?"

Although Mrs. Castellucci's claim to being related to Michelangelo Buonarroti had been checked by genealogical experts and found to be true, Vatican officials did not answer her letter. One Italian critic chose to explain the Vatican's silence this way: "The Pope economizes and saves his company three hundred lire!"

Among the Italians, particularly among the residents

of Rome, the Vatican has a reputation for being "cheap," "tight," "stingy." Without much provocation, the ordinary man in the street is likely to tell you, *Il Vaticano riceve—ma non da a nessuno!* (The Vatican receives—but gives to no one!) This is not true, of course. For the Roman Catholic Church is a practicing charitable institution—it receives charity; and it gives charity. In recent years especially, the Pope has made it a practice to allot gifts to countries hit by natural disasters, even where the people concerned are not Roman Catholics. These gifts have regularly been five-figure ones, most of them from $10,000 to $50,000. There is no way of ascertaining just how much money the Pope gives away in such outright grants, because the Vatican does not make the outlay public. Moreover, the Vatican offers little or no information about how much money it spends each year or each month. But it is known that there are sizable monthly expenditures.

To run any kind of business, to run a country of any size, large amounts of money must be spent. Running the Vatican is no exception. During one of his rare press conferences, the late Cardinal Tardini revealed the fact that the Vatican's annual payroll came to about $7.25 million. It wasn't clear, however, whether this figure referred only to the payroll for the State of Vatican City. Most likely it did, because veteran Vaticanologists are inclined to estimate the pope's total expenses at somewhere close to $20 million a year.

What are some of the costs incurred annually by the Vatican? Those of keeping its huge palaces, offices, and residential buildings in repair, painted, and heated, and of having its spacious gardens groomed by a staff of lay workers. Those of maintaining a private army, the Swiss

154

Guards and the Gendarmery, of about two hundred men, who receive some $260,000 in pay, according to rank and arm. Those of providing funds for an extensive diplomatic corps, including papal "ambassadors" in over eighty countries. Those of maintaining St. Peter's Basilica and St. Peter's Square, which alone must run to approximately $700,000 a year, of keeping a fleet of sixty cars in running order, of operating a powerful radio station, and of printing a newspaper six days a week. Churchmen, from cardinals down to ushers, must be paid. So must staff Latinists, throne bearers, lawyers, librarians, and myriads of others who provide their services inside and outside—and upon—the Leonine Walls, which, solid and thick as they are, need constant attention by a special crew of stonemasons.

Low as salaries are within the Vatican, no overtime is ever paid. Unharassed by unions, and not given to extravagance, the Vatican nevertheless granted several recent pay hikes. At the present time, a cardinal on the Pope's immediate staff draws a monthly salary of $650, plus a $100 housing allowance if he lives outside Vatican City. If a cardinal also heads a congregation, he is allowed an additional $50. Thus some prelates earn salaries as high as $800 each month. This figure does not include donations and fees given to—and kept by—cardinals for lending their presence at such special events as weddings, funerals, and the laying of cornerstones.

The Vatican payroll reflects favoritism toward any married worker who has children. For instance, a gardener receives a base wage of $115 a month, but if he has four dependent children, his monthly salary is increased to $195. A Vatican usher in the lowest category receives, after ten years' service, $235 a month; the editor

155

of the daily paper draws $340, while a printer gets $120; a private in the Swiss Guards gets a monthly $120 and his food and board. Each of these employees is awarded an extra $20 a month for every child, with no limit imposed as to the number of children (or bonuses). Altogether there are some three thousand persons who draw paychecks from the pontifical treasury.

It was Pope John XXIII who awarded salary increases to Vatican employees, and in doing so, revealed his compassionate nature. Given to taking long afternoon strolls in the Vatican Gardens, the Pope never liked the fact that all the workers scurried away from him. One day when a group of path sweepers fled as he neared them, the Pope insisted that the men come out of their hiding places behind the bushes. One by one they emerged, timidly approached the pontiff, and went to their knees. But John was not one for ceremony; he asked the men about their families, and after several had boasted of their children, and of how many of them they had, he asked how much sweepers were paid for their work.

"What?" the Pope exclaimed when he heard that a day's pay came to only 1,000 lire ($1.60). "No family with children can live on that. What has become of justice? Just wait . . . that's going to change!"

The Pope went immediately to his office to get the full facts about his employees' pay scale. On his order, a general review of all Vatican wages and salaries was made. Apprised of the figures, the Pope then ordered an across-the-board salary increase.

When he announced the new salary schedule, John told Vatican administrators, "We cannot always require others to observe the Church's teaching on social justice if we do not apply it in our own domain. The Church must take the lead in social justice by its own good example."

The pay raise, the first in many years, added an estimated $2.4 million a year to Vatican payroll expenses. Then in 1963, Pope Paul VI granted another raise, 20 percent to the entire staff. This increased the Vatican's annual salary costs by another $1.44 million. It must be mentioned here that whenever such pay hikes are granted, the Vatican grants concomitant raises, in the form of "adjustments," to former employees (civilian workers, not clergy) on pension. In another unprecedented move, Pope Paul, in December 1965, ordered that a special 100,000-lire ($160) bonus be paid to all Vatican staff to mark the successful end of the Ecumenical Council. This sum was over and above the *tredicesimo,* or thirteenth, an annual extra month's pay that Italian law requires employers to give each employee.

The Vatican wage scale may be low by American standards, but the almost unbelievable fact about the papal payroll is that the Pope himself receives not a penny in salary. Therefore, when a ranking cardinal wins election to the pontifical seat, he earns a much-esteemed promotion—with a substantial reduction in pay.

Popes have had varying amounts of personal wealth, but probably no pope has had as little as Pope John. Before he assumed the papal throne, Cardinal Roncalli managed to get together enough money for his family to buy back the house in which he and his brothers had been born so that the Roncalli relatives could once again live under the same roof. Dr. Piero Mazzoni, the Roman physician who attended Pope John in his dying days, discovered that a fountain pen was one of John's very few personal possessions of value.

"You have done much for me," the peasant-like pontiff whispered to Dr. Mazzoni on his deathbed. "Take this pen—it's all I have with which to repay you for your care and devotion. It's almost new; I've hardly ever used it."

The only other tangible possession John left behind was his pectoral cross, which he gave to Franz Cardinal Koenig, Archbishop of Vienna, who wears it at special events.

But personal funds are not a papal concern. It's the Vatican's expenses that engage popes in battles with the ledgers. To meet unforeseen expenses, the Vatican sometimes has to "rob Peter to pay Paul," in the figurative sense, of course. During the final months of the Ecumenical Council, for example, the Vatican sold $4.5 million in gold to the United States government. The bills accrued by the council required dollar payments. For one thing, the Vatican had to pay transportation costs for most of the 2,200 prelates who had to travel long distances to take their council seats each session. Most of the representatives came on foreign airlines, which required payment in American dollars; the Vatican had to come up with $2.12 million for that expense alone. Additional outlays included those for electronic calculators and special precision devices. These were supplied by non-Italian companies, which would not accept Italian lire in payment. The $4.5 million did not, of course, represent the total cost of underwriting the Ecumenical Council. Miscellaneous expenses—foremost of which was the installation of a meeting hall on the floor of St. Peter's —amounted to a staggering $7.2 million. A precise accounting of the expenses run up by the Ecumenical Council cannot be made—but speculations have placed the total between $20 and $30 million.

Apart from such special expenses as those of the Ecumenical Council, the Vatican treasury is constantly drained by the Church-sponsored organization that, with its staff of hundreds, spreads the Catholic religion to remote corners of the globe. This organization, known as the Congregation for the Evangelization of Nations or the Congregation for the Propagation of the Faith (known, too, by its Latin name, *Propaganda Fide*), was founded by Pope Gregory XV to attend to the financial requirements of Vatican missionaries. Operating in the red, because it will not take financial aid from the natives it serves, *Propaganda Fide* relies fully and completely on the Vatican's pecuniary resources. While special collections are made in Catholic churches everywhere to help *Propaganda Fide,* and while a considerable sum is raised through this source, the Vatican still has to draw liberally on its own funds to make up deficits. Although the Vatican is known to be masterful in the practice of economy measures, it pours millions of dollars into its missions every year.

Does taking on such indebtedness have any justification in the Vatican scheme of things? *Propaganda Fide* missions are in most of Africa and in large portions of Asia. Although the number of colonial areas has been diminishing, the Catholic population of the mission territories has jumped by fifteen million in the last ten years and is now estimated at forty-five million. Much of this increase in population can be attributed to the creation of native priests and the naming of Asiatics and black Africans to high posts within the Vatican structure. The number of native-born priests in Africa, Asia, and the South Sea islands has increased by more than six thousand in the last twenty-five years, while the number of

European priests in these territories has gone down by a third during the same period, according to the latest statistics. In the early nineteen-twenties, Africa and Asia had one native bishop; there are now seventy-five in Asia and about forty in Africa. The Vatican is willing to absorb the costs of the missionary army in order to achieve its purposes, even though, from a money standpoint, the loss is a total one.

Propaganda Fide is but one of the Vatican's money-losing operations. Most of its charitable undertakings are under the wing of the Congregation for the Clergy (formerly called the Congregation of the Council), which administers such projects as the financing of new schools and hospitals to replace those that have been destroyed by natural catastrophes. Wherever a poor parish needs financial help, the Congregation for the Clergy stands ready to give aid, usually in the form of money. Ordinarily the Vatican does not provide succor to specific individuals, but upon occasion it may help a parish priest to get certain poor families back on their feet. The amount spent on this type of assistance is unknown, but the figure is surely sizable. Another organization that makes heavy demands on Vatican resources is Vatican Radio, the official station of the Holy See. The station broadcasts in Latin and thirty other languages and relays many programs to countries behind the Iron Curtain. On a given day, the powerful Vatican transmitters may beam two shows to Hungary, two to Czechoslovakia, and three to Rumania. In the course of a week, there will be four broadcasts in Byelorussian, three in Ukrainian, two in Bulgarian, and a half a dozen in the various Yugoslav dialects. Most of the broadcasts, however, are in Italian (with English in second place, for Far Eastern audiences). Newscasts on the Pope's activities, special church ceremonies, masses, religious music, and papal messages are transmitted on twenty-four short-wave and three medium-wave bands, and are heard all over the world. The transmitters, which cost $3 million, are located on the highest ground in the Vatican Gardens and in a walled-in, two-mile-square plot north of Rome, which has been given extraterritorial status.

Unknown to most people, even regular listeners to Vatican Radio, is the fact that during the early morning hours of each day the office of the Vatican's secretary of state broadcasts messages—some of them in code—to priests, nuncios, apostolic delegates, and cardinals in all parts of the world. Each Church dignitary knows about what time to expect special announcements pertaining to his region. He also receives coded signals from the Vatican to remind him of the "date" he has with his receiver.

In contrast with other stations, Vatican Radio often communicates private messages that will not be understood by anyone but the papal representative for whom they are intended. One might, for instance, hear something like this: "Father Tizio, with reference to the information in your letter of the eighth of September, re the peasant woman who sees visions of the Virgin Mary, we have considered your suggestion, but suggest that *ad captandum vulgus. . . .*"

Several years ago, when N.B.C. correspondent Irving R. Levine visited the station and was told that there was such a daily transmission to the United States, he asked in jest, "Is that when Cardinal Spellman gets his orders from the Vatican?"

The staff member who was acting as Levine's guide

replied with a grin, "No, sir, it's just the other way around!"

Vatican Radio is a significant papal expense; so, too, is the unofficial Vatican newspaper. An eight- to ten-page evening paper printed six times a week, *L'Osservatore Romano* sells at 60 lire (10 cents) a copy on newsstands. An annual subscription in Italy costs $25, whereas, for copies that go abroad, the subscription rate comes to $40 a year. An incredibly dull publication, it has virtually no newsstand sales, but it does have a paid mail circulation of about fifty thousand copies, including four that are sent by air to Moscow. Issued in Italian, it frequently contains several columns in Latin, and it will often print speeches and reprint documents in the German, English, French, Spanish, or Portuguese in which they were first delivered or printed. The paper carries a very small amount of advertising and almost never runs photographs.

L'Osservatore operates at a loss of $2 million a year, and, despite the paper's importance to the Vatican, this fact disturbed Pope Pius XII.

Pius, who tended to be a penny-wise-pound-foolish administrator, diligently watched every penny the Vatican spent. To save on electric current, for instance, Pius often made the rounds of the papal apartments flicking off the lights. Not infrequently he refused to make necessary repairs because he didn't want to spend the money. "I cannot," he said, "be extravagant with the funds of the Holy See."

It was Pius XII who established the Vatican policy of reusing envelopes. Intra-Vatican communications were not to be sealed in such a way that the envelope could not be used again. It was also Pius who wrote his last will and testament on the back of an envelope that had made the rounds—and who once discovered, to his chagrin, that he had a drawerful of obsolete bank notes that would have been worth close to $1,000 if he hadn't neglected to turn them in before the government's redemption deadline.

Scandals,
Scandals . . .
XII

POSSIBLY THE LEAST understood spot on the globe is the Italian island of Sicily, which is noted chiefly for its exportation of gangsters to the United States.

Sicily is a world unto itself, a world in which people live in wretched poverty. The Vatican has a formidable stake in this miserably depressed area, a fact that sometimes forces the clergy to join hands with the Mafia.

In Italy you are friends if you have the same enemies —and in Sicily a forty-four-year-old poet and architect from the "hated north" has emerged as the nemesis of both the Vatican and the Mafia. Known as the Sicilian Gandhi, Danilo Dolci of Trieste has already become something of a legendary hero. He is also one of the most hated men in Italy.

Although powerful, his enemies—the dreaded Mafia, the powerful Sicilian landowners, and the Vatican—have not been able to destroy him. For if there is hatred for Danilo Dolci in the most influential Italian circles, there is unbounded admiration for him outside Italy. His dramatic work among the Sicilian poor has drawn hundreds of volunteer pilgrims from Sweden, Switzerland, and England—people who pay their own expenses for the privilege of working with the gentle, round-faced rebel.

Sixteen years ago, Danilo Dolci was, at twenty-eight, a successful architect, the author of two architectural books, and a respected man in his field. Then he made a tour of Sicily, saw the appalling ignorance, apathy, and misery of the people—and decided to abandon his profession. He settled down in the fishing village of Trapetto, married a semiliterate widow with five children, and after adopting five more children, began using Mahatma Gandhi's nonviolent methods to campaign for social reforms.

The first battle was fought with a hunger strike. Widely publicized, it brought some help to Trapetto. The next battle, however, brought the police. Dolci had rounded up two hundred unemployed men to work without pay on a road that needed repairs for which the Christian Democratic government seemed unable to delegate funds. Dolci led what was in effect a "strike in reverse," for when the police ordered him to desist, he and his helpers calmly continued with their work. Infuriated, the police arrested him for "trespassing on public property." In Palermo he was tried on five counts and sentenced to seven weeks in prison.

The nature of the "crime" and the ludicrous aspects of the trial resulted in unprecedented publicity. Before long, spontaneous Danilo Dolci committees sprouted up all over Europe and began to send money. Italian politicians were embarrassed, and when Dolci accepted the Lenin Prize for a volume of poetry, they tried to dismiss him as a Communist agent.

But financial aid still reaches Dolci, and foreign pilgrims still come to work with him. And Dolci is creating some minor miracles. He has built a shelter, known as the Village of God, for orphans and destitute families. He's also dammed a small river to provide irrigation, built two modest-sized hospitals and a pharmacy, and constructed many sewers and roads. After moving his headquarters from Trapetto to the larger town of Partinico, which he considered a bigger challenge, he began, with forty foreign volunteers, a program to teach the peasants how to use new farming methods and to develop new crops.

In recent years, Dolci has been using long sit-down strikes in various small hill towns of western Sicily. In the fall of 1963, for example, Dolci staged a nine-day fast and mass sit-down in front of the only church in the town of Roccamena. Joining in the protest were movie star Vittorio Gassman and author Carlo Levi. Intellectuals from other European countries also joined the six hundred townsfolk and spent entire nights sitting and sleeping outdoors on straw mats. Gassman occasionally provided entertainment by reciting passages from Dante's *Divine Comedy* while standing in the glare of auto headlights.

At issue was the Bruca Dam. The project had been delayed by Christian Democratic politicians for thirty years. Rome had earmarked $12.8 million for the Bruca Dam in 1952, but the money had disappeared, and work was never begun. The earlier $1.6 million that the government had appropriated for preliminary work had also vanished. So Roccamena remained without water, and its people were left to try to scratch a living from their arid but potentially fertile soil. The little water available was used for the advantage of the wealthy few, who had the support of the Vatican and the Mafia, while millions of gallons of water from the unharnessed Belice River ran off and was wasted. As the Dolci sit-in headlines mounted, so, too, did the pressure on Rome. At long last, the Ministry of Public Works conceded and issued an order to begin work on the Bruca Dam.

Situations like that in Roccamena often develop because Vatican strategies are based on a belief that it is easier for the Church to maintain its strength where poverty, misery, and ignorance breed. Italy's southland is a case in point. Ironically, the situation is aggravated by the Cassa per il Mezzogiorno (Southland Development Fund), which, instead of bringing economic relief to an insular backyard like Sicily, has become a gigantic patronage organization. Often, developmental contracts are awarded strictly on the basis of political considerations —one of the most important of which is loyalty to the Christian Democratic party. Because the practice is no secret, bishops and local politicians have little trouble impressing recalcitrant individuals with the fact that there is little to be gained from supporting activities not approved by the Vatican.

The system is so firmly entrenched that it is not surprising to find many people who believe that Sicily, despite its formal governmental machinery, is nothing more than a Vatican holding. People have been shaking their heads over the situation for years, but until Danilo Dolci came on the scene, the combined forces of the old nobility, the Mafia, and the Church had escaped meaningful opposition. Dolci, a professed Roman Catholic who never attends mass, puts into practice the humanitarian ideas of the Church; the Vatican opposes him not on philosophical or theological grounds, but on hard business principles. Because of Dolci, there is danger that the Vatican's

167

most valuable resource—its churchgoing believers—may be diminished.

Paradoxically, Dolci is well liked by the local priests, who know him personally, and he is held in some admiration by Mafia chiefs, who, for reasons of their own, have left him alone. In Sicily it is said that if Dolci has not been assassinated by now, he never will be.

Dolci, who asks no quarter in his struggles against the Catholic hierarchy, is disliked in papal circles and is considered a thorn in the side of the Christian Democratic party. He is often accused of flirting with Communism and opening the way to a red-backed renaissance in Sicily. But his encounters with the mainland *democristiani* are largely ignored by the Vatican, which does not want to elevate him by engaging in a direct confrontation.

But if the Vatican has preferred to avoid a collision with Dolci, the Bank of Sicily (Banco di Sicilia) has chosen another course. The bank, a financial arm of the pope, is the overseer of the Vatican's holdings in the western end of Sicily and, as such, has tried without marked success to make short shrift of the so-called Sicilian Gandhi. A recent scandal within the bank has reduced some of the pressures on Dolci.

Carlo Bazan, the bank's highly respected president, was arrested in 1967 on charges of alleged irregularities. Over an eight-year period, he had hired nearly a hundred members of his family to fill various key posts in the bank —and, while nepotism is not unknown in Palermo and does not necessarily constitute a legal offense, Bazan, thrust into the glare of an unfavorable spotlight, was accused of having doctored records and overlooked payments due on loans made to members of his family.

Postwar Italy has been rife with scandals. Perhaps no

more but certainly no less than any other power institution in Italy, the Vatican has had its share of troubles in this respect. But because of the Vatican's position and prestige, foreign correspondents in Rome, and all too many Italian newspapermen also, have remained silent, or almost so.

Two recent subjects of scandal—the Fiumicino airport and the price of bananas—deserve more attention than they have received.

There are whole generations of Italians that don't know what a good banana—a *real* banana—tastes like. Italy's banana scandal made headlines inside Italy but caused no stir outside its borders, mostly because of the protective attitude of Rome's resident correspondents toward the Catholic Church.

"La camorra delle banane" (the banana racket) began innocently enough. On December 2, 1935, while Italy was at war with Ethiopia, the *Gazzetta Ufficiale* published a decree that announced a new state monopoly—on the sale of bananas. Italy's merchant ships were charged with the responsibility of transporting bananas from Libya, Somalia, and the Italian-owned islands of the Aegean. Up to that time, under a system of free enterprise, bananas had been exported to Italy not only by its colonies but also by the Canary Islands, by the Antilles, and by Guinea. Altogether, these last countries had raised their banana exports to Italy almost 200 percent, from eleven million pounds in 1925 to nearly thirty-one million in 1934. Bananas from Somalia in 1925 represented only 2 percent of Italy's total banana imports, but by 1955 the Italian colony, through favoritism, had garnered better

169

than 83 percent of the banana trade with Italy, having reached a total of close to eighty million pounds.

The establishment of the new Italian monopoly was more a political move than an economic one. It was designed to help the Italians establish themselves as "colonizers" in Africa by developing trade between the colonies and the mother country. The African bananas were an unsound economic proposition in the general European market, for it cost too much to produce them, too much to ship them, and, what's more, they were of inferior quality. To administer the new monopoly, the Italian government set up a special agency, Regia Azienda Monopolio Banane (R.A.M.B.), which purchased the bananas from the growers and stabilized the prices with the middlemen and the retailers.

According to the terms of the decree, R.A.M.B. was supposed to put up for public bid concessions for forty-eight wholesalers, each of whom would have a specified territory. But, between 1937 and 1940, R.A.M.B. "temporarily" assigned these concessions—until a public competition could be held. The forty-eight persons who received the supposedly temporary concessions were high-ranking Fascists and Vatican-endorsed men and their relatives. These agents retained their concessions during the forties, the fifties, and the middle sixties.

In February 1945, the Minister of the Treasury dissolved R.A.M.B. and nominated a special commission to study the sale of bananas. After nine years, during which an emergency committee of R.A.M.B. continued administering the sale of bananas while the special committee undertook the inquiry, a new government agency was set up to deal with the banana monopoly. It was called l'Azienda da Monopolio Banane (A.M.B.), and

170

what it was was essentially only the old Regia Azienda Monopolio Banane with a new name and a new set of identifying initials.

A.M.B., in one of its first acts, raised the number of concessions from forty-eight to eighty-six. All eighty-six concessions were to be good for only one year; then the public was to be given a chance to bid on them. The public competition never took place, however, and the eighty-six concessionaires continued to hold their assigned territories.

A.M.B., in another of its first acts, established a fixed price for bananas in the wholesale and retail markets. Although the price of bananas in other countries fluctuated with the season, the price in Italy remained the same throughout the year. And the retail price of a colonial banana in Italy was over twice the price of a banana from the Canary Islands or Spanish Africa in other European countries. Thanks to A.M.B., Italians had to pay 475 lire (approximately 77 cents) for a kilogram of bananas; in nearby France a kilo of bananas cost half of that—even when the fruit was in short supply.

To add to the injury, Somalian bananas were of inferior commercial quality. No other country would import them. But Italy did and, thanks to A.M.B., paid a wholesale price of 106 lire a kilo for them—at a time when the highest wholesale price being paid for superior bananas was the equivalent (in pesos, francs, and other European currencies) of only 50 lire a kilo.

It should also be pointed out that the banana growers were getting 18 to 20 lire a kilo from the Italian "banana handlers" who resold the bananas to A.M.B. at the fixed 106-lire price. These "banana handlers"—theoretically serving on foreign soil—actually did not live outside Italy, nor did they ever see any of the bananas they were "handling." They transacted their business at the Via Veneto sidewalk cafés, lived in Rome's posh Parioli district, and kept summer villas at Viareggio on the Costa Azzurra.

Because of their "understanding" with A.M.B., the so-called banana handlers netted the equivalent of $4 million a year more than they would have netted in a freely competitive situation. Owners of the merchant boats that brought the bananas to Italy's ports also had a deal with A.M.B.—and were making an extra $2.4 million a year. Local wholesale distributors were taking in an extra $3.84 million, and retailers an extra $4.48 million. Thus a grand total of $14.72 million—extra—was "earned" by individuals connected with Italy's banana business. But not all of this money stayed in their pockets; a percentage was given to certain *pezzi grossi* (literally, big pieces—Italian slang for bigshots) who were affiliated with the Christian Democratic party.

Despite the artificially inflated prices paid by the Italian people (who never realized what people in other countries were paying for bananas), the sale of bananas in Italy almost quintupled over a twelve-year period—rising from 56.2 million pounds in 1951 to over 279.3 million in 1963.

And, in 1960, to add to the irony, Italy's finance minister bestowed silver and bronze medals on the banana concessionaires for the fine work they had been doing over the years. Three years later, the decorated individuals were indicted on charges of having committed fraud in the handling and sale of bananas. That was in 1963 —the trials still have not come up.

Gathering dust in the archives of Italy's newspapers are reports of other financial scandals, involving Rome's gleaming multimillion-dollar Leonardo da Vinci Airport. In the archives of non-Italian newspapers, there is nothing, or almost nothing, about these scandals, for the fuss over the Leonardo da Vinci International Airport at Fiumicino received very little coverage outside Italy. One American newsman confided to me that he had filed some good copy on the subject, but his editor in New York had told him to "lay off." Which he did.

When the story broke in 1961, I was representing McGraw-Hill's technical news weeklies and was able to cable full details from Rome. Which were printed. Subscribers to *Aviation Week* and *Engineering News-Record* were thus kept abreast of the Fiumicino airport situation. But very few newspaper readers in the United States learned the deplorable, almost incredible facts.

In 1952, the city of Rome recognized that its airport at Ciampino would soon be inadequate. Ciampino, which was ideally located, had three runways, each of them 7,380 feet long. Each could have been extended to accommodate jet planes, for the airport was situated in an uninhabited area with plenty of available lands. But, instead of allocating funds for Ciampino's expansion, the Italian government elected to buy up large parcels of land in the nearby coastal town of Fiumicino.

As an airport site, Fiumicino had nothing to recommend it. A marshland near the mouth of the Tiber, it had earlier (in 1944) been rejected by the United States Army Air Force as a landing field for bombers. The Air Force report stated that shifting sands, frequent fogs, and occasional flooding made the land somewhat less than ideal for an airport site. Nevertheless, the Italian government paid $21 million for it. The purchase was made after the site had been recommended to the government by the Vatican-owned Società Generale Immobiliare.

173

Prince Torlonia, who was prominent in many Catholic organizations, and whose family was prominent in Vatican history, received for the land the equivalent of $1,300 a hectare (about $525 an acre), even though at nearby Casal Palocco a huge parcel of fog-free, flood-free land was available for sale at considerably less.

Had the existing airport at Ciampino been expanded, or had the available Casal Palocco land been purchased, the government would not have had to appropriate $7.2 million to shore up the shifting sands of Fiumicino in order to lay concrete for the runways. It took workmen at Fiumicino five years to control the sand. Often their labors were interrupted by heavy fogs that descended over the site. Fogs are still a problem at Fiumicino—so much of a problem that airport authorities frequently have to direct traffic to the old Ciampino field.

All of this skulduggery took place before Rome came around to recognizing, in 1952, that Ciampino Airport would no longer do, but the scandal of Fiumicino had not yet reached the front pages. The purchase of the Torlonia land had been carried out quietly, even though $21 million in public funds had been spent. As it developed, the $21 million was a mere drop in the bucket.

On January 15, 1955, the Italian government allocated $22.4 million "for the prosecution and completion of an international airport at Rome, by the Ministry of Public Works, to include such necessary other works as connecting roadways to the city limits, electrical installations, and a communications system." Although three plans had been submitted, the Ministry of Public Works did not select any of them and, a year later (January 13, 1956), asked for the sum of $10.4 million to study some new projects for the airport. Three more years went by, and on April 28, 1959, the Ministry of Public Works asked for, and got, the sum of $6.64 million "to make the airport operative." Three months later another $640,000 was allocated "for the prosecution and completion of the work." Other special allocations had been granted along the way—$1.76 million for Ministry expenses accruing from the building of the airport, $8 million for connecting roadways to the city limits, and $6.4 million for debts the Ministry had accumulated because of the airport. All this money was granted *a singhiozzi* (hiccup style), in violation of an Italian law that clearly states that all financial allocations for public works of an extraordinary nature must be discussed by the parliament and that a bill must be passed for any withdrawals from the treasury. The appropriation of money for the airport was certainly irregular. There were to be further irregularities.

The contract to construct the runways was awarded to the Manfredi Construction Company. It is no small coincidence that Manfredi belonged to the Vatican. The contract to build the main terminal was put up for public bidding, in which eight construction companies participated. Provera e Carrassi, the Vatican-owned company that won the bid at $5.12 million, proceeded to build the terminal building, but on the 376th day of work discovered that it had "underestimated" the total cost. Without further ado, or any publicity, the sum paid to Provera e Carrassi was raised another $4.38 million. Not until the final accounting was made was it learned that Provera e Carrassi had received 80 percent over its "low bid."

A contract was given to the Castelli Construction Company (also Vatican owned) to put up the hangars. The sum of money earmarked for this expense was listed on the budget at $4.54 million. On the final expense sheet, however, it was not possible to determine just how much Castelli was paid for the work. So, too, with the amount paid the Vaselli Company, another Vatican-owned company, which got the assignment of building the connecting roadways.

If this sounds like the making of a good scandal, that's precisely what it turned out to be in the spring of 1961. Although the world press generally ignored the details, the Italian press gave them adequate attention. The coverage was particularly full in Rome's left-wing evening daily, *Paese Sera,* which printed a series of documented articles. The articles named names.

The Christian Democratic government set up a legislative commission to probe the matter, and, although four ministers (all Christian Democrats) were cited for irregularities in the report to the President of the Senate and the Chamber of Deputies, no criminal charges were made. Since the special investigating commission was primarily intended to placate an indignant Italian citizenry, the only person who finally received any kind of punishment was a small-time colonel in the Ministry of Defense. His punishment took the form of a transfer from an office in Rome to a post in Bari, on the other side of the peninsula.

During its first years the Leonardo da Vinci International Airport had its problems. It still has problems. Because of the settlement of the fill and the impact of giant jet liners, the main runway developed cracks—some of them over a mile long—that had to be repaved. The three-story terminal building, made entirely of glass, has neither windows that open nor air conditioning. On warm days it tends to be unpleasant, to say the least. In cold weather it's not much better, for radiant heat pipes just below the surface of the rubber floor send up acrid fumes of seared rubber. Combine these with the jet fumes that hang motionless in the nonventilated terminal, and one understands why some travelers become ill from the smell.

So much for the terminal building. As for the airport as a whole, some Italians, knowing its history, don't like the stench.

Prophets
and
Profits
XIII

"In the Vatican everything is forbidden, and everything is possible."

(Vatican saying)

IN THE SPRING of 1958, the Vatican became the victim of a "hat trick." A publicist by the name of Guido Orlando was hired by the Millinery Institute of America, which wanted him to promote the sales of women's hats. Orlando accomplished his task by pulling a stunt that involved Pope Pius XII.

Thinking (correctly, it turned out) that canon law, which requires women to cover their heads at services, might somehow be used to boost women's hat sales, Orlando set about trying to get the Pope to make an official pronouncement stating that hats were a proper part of women's dress. Toward this end, Orlando created the Religious Institute of Research, which forthwith announced the "results of a survey" indicating that over twenty million women in North America attended mass every week without their heads covered. The statistics were phony, of course, as was the letterhead of the Religious Institute of Research on which Orlando communicated the news of the "research" to His Holiness.

The letter suggested that the pontiff urge women to

178

attend religious services dressed according to established rule, and thereby preserve the tradition of the Church. Boldly, Orlando added, "The remarks I thought Your Holiness might make could be phrased, 'Of the various pieces of apparel worn by women today, hats do the most to enhance the dignity and decorum of womanhood. It is traditional for hats to be worn by women in church and at other religious occasions, and I commend hats as a right and proper part of women's dress.' "

Aggressive though this was, it worked. A short while later, during a public audience, Pope Pius incorporated Orlando's very words into a general recommendation that women wear hats. *L'Osservatore Romano* ran the story, which was then picked up by the wire services and the foreign correspondents. Most of the daily newspapers in the United States and Canada gave it space. The Pope's quotation went on display in many hat-store windows, printed on large posters. Within a month there was a sharp upturn in the sales of women's hats—and the Pope in his palace may have wondered about the questionable ethics of the world outside.

Today the world outside has comparatively little trouble getting into the inner recesses of the Vatican. Reaching the Pope is no longer a near impossibility, and the path Orlando took to get to His Holiness seems devious indeed. Today, a mere decade later, there is a new Vatican; many changes have taken place, and are taking place. These changes began to manifest themselves when the second Ecumenical Council met for its first sessions, in October 1962. Pope John himself established the keynote when a Church official asked him just what purpose the council was supposed to serve. Walking over to his study window and pushing it open, he answered, "That's

179

what the council's purpose is supposed to be—to let some fresh air into the Church!"

Every pope has his own method of bringing "fresh air" into his administration. New popes have a way of cleaning house once they shed their cardinal's robes and move into the papal chambers of the Apostolic Palace. So it was with the present pontiff, Paul VI, after he took over in June of 1963.

Pope Paul brought with him some personal belongings, set up a favorite desk and chairs, and installed his own comfortable bed. In addition, he wanted to bring a "new look" to his Vatican apartment—and amazed everybody in the enclave when he ordered the eighteen marble busts of previous popes which lined the palace's private antechambers to be taken away and stored for safekeeping. Then he had the old damask and red brocade stripped from the walls in order to achieve a more modern decor. Local artists were summoned to redo the private pontifical chapel. At Paul's request, bombproof storage cells were constructed to house many Vatican treasures beneath the lawns of the Vatican Gardens.

Also at Paul's request, two great halls at Belvedere Court were readied to accommodate the new senate of bishops with which he would be meeting from time to time as a result of the Second Ecumenical Council. Another new assembly room seating twelve thousand people was fixed up to provide space for the overflow at papal audiences. In addition, Paul brought in new equipment —electronic brains, electric generators, modern switchboards, and the latest in public-address systems.

"The Church is not a museum of memories," he declared. "It is a living community."

This is the attitude one encounters in Vatican City

today. It is the recognition that the Church, however slowly, is changing in many of its aspects. It is the awareness that if the future is to hold any promise of perpetuity for the Vatican, the Church must indeed change.

Religion in general, and Catholicism in particular, is on the decline in the twentieth century. Catholicism cannot hope to thrive much longer on the credulous imagination of immature populaces. Quietly, Vatican leaders are coming to grips with the realization that religion is stronger in the more backward areas. With its nineteen centuries of experience, the Church—which purports to know about the next world—displays a great deal of knowledge about this one, too, and is doing a nuts-and-bolts job of taking care of itself.

The contemporary decline of religious belief in many parts of the globe, a phenomenon that has followed in the wake of industrialization, political sophistication, and scientific and educational progress, spells trouble for the Vatican as a religious institution. And the Vatican knows it. But the Vatican is more than a religious institution, more than a political institution. It is a solid economic entity, firmly entrenched in the world of business and finance.

As a "big business," the Vatican considers Communism its great enemy. Necessarily this could mean a fight to the finish between the Church of Rome and the "Church of Moscow." Let no one have any doubts about the Vatican. It is afraid of the Communists, deathly afraid. There is, of course, the fact that Communism preaches atheism, but the greater danger lies in the financial sphere. Had the Communists successfully taken over Italy in the 1948 election, private enterprise would have ceased. And virtually every penny the Vatican had invested in Italy's economy would have been confiscated by the state.

Heavy with the memory of centuries, the Vatican takes the long view on matters of immediate importance to its survival. One can discern, even from afar, the Vatican's eagerness to pull the checkstring on Communism by bringing Catholicism to other continents. The creation of Asiatic and African cardinals and the escalation of efforts in the missionary countries, particularly in the development of a "native clergy," are part of the global strategy being used by the Vatican. Not surprisingly, the Church wants to establish itself in non-European and non-American lands.

Perhaps more important, however, is the Church's role as an economic force. Here again the Vatican's emphasis is on survival—by meeting the enemy (Communism) head on. Having long ago formed "alliances" with Wall Street and other financial nerve centers, the Vatican stands ready to wield an economic sword in the "crusade" against godless Communism.

To counteract the danger of Moscow and Peking, the Vatican will support, in substance if not in theory, the methods of doing business in the United States. Unable to accept Marxist principles that represent a strong threat to its future security, the Vatican created a sort of no-man's-land between itself and the Kremlin; today, however, in a move to delimit the influence of the Communists, the Vatican is embarking on a mission to "make friends" with its deadly enemy. Consequently, it is facing one of the gravest dilemmas in its history. There are a great many blueprints for containing Communism, and each of them has its pitfalls, but the Vatican has a multi-billion-dollar investment to protect, and behind the

182

scenes, is preparing for a life under a system of international security which necessarily involves some kind of working relationship with the other side. It is for this reason that in the sixties Pope John and his successor, Pope Paul, sought a settlement that would guarantee the future for both sides.

In the spring of 1967, Pope Paul expressed some wide-ranging views on the world's social situation in his encyclical *Populorum Progressio* (*On the Development of Peoples*). The Pope declared that "the introduction of industry is a necessity for economic growth and human progress." But on the subject of "liberal capitalism," he added:

> It is unfortunate that in these new conditions of society a system has been constructed which considers profit as the key motive for economic progress, competition as the supreme law of economics, and private ownership of the means of production as an absolute right that has no limits and carries no corresponding social obligation. This unchecked liberalism leads to dictatorship.
>
> One cannot condemn such abuses too strongly by solemnly recalling once again that the economy is at the service of man.
>
> But if it is true that a type of capitalism has been the source of excessive suffering, injustices, and fratricidal conflicts whose effects still persist, it would also be wrong to attribute to industrialization itself evils that belong to the woeful system which accompanied it.
>
> On the contrary, one must recognize in all justice the irreplaceable contribution made by the organization of labor and of industry to what development has accomplished.
>
> Private property does not constitute for anyone an absolute and unconditional right. No one is justified in keeping for his exclusive use what he does not need, when others lack necessities.

Speaking with a great sense of urgency, the Pope called for a far-reaching plan to bring economic progress and social improvement to the underdeveloped nations. He urged all men of good will to unite in an effort to end the world's misery, adding that rich nations must give greater aid to poor ones. Studiously vague, the encyclical maintained that central economic planning is the key to economic development, that free markets and private enterprise have at most a minor role to play.

"Individual initiative alone and the mere free play of competition," said Pope Paul, "could never assure successful development. . . . It pertains to the public authorities to choose, even to lay down, the objectives to be pursued, the ends to be achieved, and the means for attaining these, and it is for them to stimulate all the forces engaged in this common activity."

Pope Paul, although well versed in the intricacies of the social sciences, and especially of sociology, preferred to ignore the subtle argument that Adam Smith espoused —that an individual "by pursuing his own interests . . . frequently promotes that of society more effectively than when he really intends to promote it."

Quite apart from any laissez-faire philosophy, the Vatican firmly subscribes to the thesis that central planning is the key to economic development. Its own financial history from 1929, when Bernardino Nogara began to run a "one-man show" with the then Italian dictator as his foil, through its profitable alliance with the Christian Democratic party has taught the Vatican some valuable lessons in the importance of maintaining careful economic control. Basically, the Pope does not endorse the view of the eighteen international businessmen and opinion leaders who offered to work with the Vatican toward world understanding of the *Populorum Progressio* encyclical and who declared in a resolution, "If the economic system is to prosper with the savings, investment, and development necessary, the state should not assume functions that can be better carried out by private initiative."

The Vatican sees its future strength in itself. Christian Democracy, which had supported a policy to promote new collective bodies toward the construction of an organized Europe, provided government leaders who were champing for, as far back as 1955, the possibility of bringing about an organization of states that would merge their national markets through the gradual abolition of customs tariffs. Some of the very first mentions of a "Common Market" came up in Messina, Sicily, in June 1955, when the Council of Foreign Ministers of the European Coal and Steel Community met. This meeting is often viewed as being the germination point of discussions that were to lead to the drafting of the Common Market Treaty that was signed in Rome on March 25, 1957. As a result of their role in the formation of the European Economic Community, the Christian Democrats have emerged as an energetic political force not only in Italy but in Western Europe as a whole. As their fortunes have risen, so too have the Vatican's. The Church today is in a healthier political and economic position than at any time in this century.

While the Vatican has remained secretive about its fiscal policy, it has never believed that the investment of Church money was either illegal, objectionable in principle, or contrary to good conscience. In seeking to resolve the conflict between that which is to be rendered to God and that which is to be rendered to Caesar, the Vatican has developed its own special *modus vivendi* between the sacred and the secular. The view of the pope as a kind of chairman of the board may shock some readers.

But let us remember that the Vatican is a remarkable, centuries-old institution, and that, when it comes to money, it is one that is fully in tune with the spirit of the times.

This writer foresees the day, perhaps a thousand years from now, when the Vatican will cease functioning as a religious institution and take up, on a full-time basis, the duties of a large-scale business corporation. The transition will not be as difficult to effectuate as one might suspect. For just as Catholicism will decline and eventually withdraw from the ranks of the major religions, so, too, will Church money find its way into nearly every area of the free world's economy. Then, at last, the tycoon on the Tiber will shed the mantle of piety; then, at last, the Vatican will expose the full extent of its financial interests.